FOUL DEEDS AND SUSPICIOUS DEATHS ON THE YORKSHIRE COAST

Foul Deeds and Suspicious Deaths on the
Yorkshire Coast

Alan Whitworth

Series Editor
Brian Elliott

Wharncliffe Books

First Published in 2001 by
Wharncliffe Books
an imprint of
Pen and Sword Books Limited,
47 Church Street, Barnsley,
South Yorkshire. S70 2AS

Copyright © Alan Whitworth

For up-to-date information on other titles produced under the
Wharncliffe imprint, please telephone or write to:

> **Wharncliffe Books**
> **FREEPOST**
> **47 Church Street**
> **Barnsley**
> **South Yorkshire S70 2BR**
> **Telephone (24 hours): 01226 - 734555**

ISBN: 1-903425-01-8

A CIP catalogue record of this book is available from the
British Library

Cover illustration: *Smugglers Attacked.* Nineteenth century (unknown artist)

Printed in the United Kingdom by
CPI UK

CONTENTS

INTRODUCTION

Violence is abhorrent to man. Yet, ironically, man is capable of great violence. It is inherent. He will defend or attack with extreme ferocity when aroused. Passions often govern these actions, whether the passion be love, hate, fear, or jealousy - and from the consequences of his violence comes the making of this book.

Foul Deeds and Suspicious Deaths on the Yorkshire Coast is a collection of true stories of murderous deeds and violent ends performed on the residents of the East Coast in particular. Possibly, indeed, probably since mankind first walked upright such deeds have been carried out whether in the form of ritual execution, spontaneous response, or cool calculation. And the manner and weapon with which the deed is often carried out can be as varied as one can possibly imagine.

Our collection begins with undoubtedly the earliest murder in the area, the death of a man in Roman times, found stabbed in the back in a coastal defensive look-out post, and beside him lay his attacker, in turn savagely killed by the victim's guard dog, his throat torn out. An open and shut case – but other murders still remain unsolved mysteries. There are also tales of smuggling, violent quarrels between seamen bent on breaking or flouting the law by trading in illegal substances and those charged with upholding the law, Revenue Officers, soldiers and the like. Pirate attacks feature too, whereupon with the capture of the pirates, they were punished most severely and often met their end in an extremely barbaric way. And there are stories of brave martyrs who were hung, drawn and quartered by the executioner. Death in such a manner is no less grisly than death by a knife in the back.

Foul Deeds and Suspicious Deaths on the Yorkshire Coast is not intended as a comprehensive catalogue of violent crimes along the East Coast. Such a catalogue would be impossible to produce as many of the area's darkest deeds are shrouded in the mists of time and folklore. It is, however, a record of select events usually ending in death, which captured the attention and imagination of our forefathers.

To some, this book might appear to border on the macabre. They would argue that many of the incidents selected for inclusion might better have been left forgotten. But closer examination of the predatory occurrences often reveals a great deal about the area and its inhabitants. They can tell us how they lived, worked and played in far greater detail than can ever be discovered from reading other forms of official records and archives.

From Roman times to the present day is the timespan which these grisly tales encompass. The murder of James Law, smuggler, at Burniston in 1823; the Vine Street murder at Scarborough in 1943; a nineteenth century murder at Cayton Bay; the murder of Mrs Cook at Marske in 1963 – babies burnt, husbands, wives, sons, lovers, soldiers, sailors murdered – they are all here, victims and perpetrators alike. A collection of grisly tales indeed, collected together for the interest and enjoyment of the innocent reader. Please enjoy.

Finally, no book such as this could have been written without the help of many people and in particular I am indebted to numerous individuals who pointed the way toward various stories and references. Especially, I should like to thank Peter Howorth for allowing the use of his article on the murder of James Law, reproduced from *Crimes and Punishments in Yorkshire 1800-37* (Lowndes Publications) and edited by me for republication in *Aspects of the Yorkshire Coast 2* (Wharncliffe Books). Also the following by name, who have assisted me greatly in my research: Mrs Enid Clarkson and the staff of Whitby Library; Mr Brian Berryman and the staff of Scarborough Local History Library; the staff of Filey Library; and Mr and Mrs Eric Pinder at the Town Council Archives, Filey. Lastly, I should mention my wife Alma, who once again gave unstinting assistance in proof reading the manuscript and making suggestions; and all the staff at Wharncliffe Books, Barnsley, for their invaluable help in production and sales.

All illustrations are from the author's own camera or collection unless otherwise acknowledged in the caption.

Horrible Murder

AND MUTILATION OF THE BODIES OF

JOSEPH WOOD AND HIS SON,

At Pickering, in the North Riding of Yorkshire, on or about the 17th or 18th of May 1872.

The above startling crime has just been brought to light by the discovery of the remains of the murdered persons, portions of whose bodies have been found in various places. The hands and feet, were found detached from the man's body, which was discovered in an old sack buried in the ground beneath an Oak Tree. The body of the poor boy has not been found, but some bones which are stated to be the remains of the poor fellow have just been discovered showing the horrible fact that his body has been devoured by the pigs on his father's farm. A man named Robert Chartre, another farmer stands committed for the murder, and has already confessed the crime.

In the quiet village of Pickering,
   Among the Yorkshire farming grounds,
A cruel murder, sad and startling,
   Has aroused the country round.
One Joseph Wood a well known farmer,
   In seclusion there did dwell.
His son and him they lived together,
   Their sad fate we now must tell.

CHORUS.

No one pities the cruel monster,
   For the deed that he has done,
Altho, he killed the poor old farmer,
   Why didn't he spare the helpless son.

These two poor victims have been missing,
   Since nearly six long months ago,
Their cruel relation, Robert Charter,
   A Liverpool letter he did show
The letter said, the poor old farmer
   And his son had gone away
From Liverpool to cross the ocean,
   And would return some other day.

There was many had their own suspicions,
   That some foul play had been done,
But nothing could be found to prove it,
   Or bring it home to the guilty one ;
At last some old shoes were discovered,
   Belonging to the missing man,
The Police were quickly made acquainted,
   And the search once more began.

They searched the fields in all directions,
   With pick and spade turned up the land,
At last beneath some muddy water,
   They saw the murder'd farmer's hand ;
They found the feet and parts of clothing,
   A sad and sick'ning sight to see,
The remainder of the decaying body
   Was buried beneath an old oak tree.

They tried to find the poor boy's body,
   They search'd around both night and day,
Human bones they have discovered,
   That ravenous pigs had gnawed away ;
The cruel monster perhaps did murder,
   The helpless unoffending boy,
And threw his body in the pigsty,
   There all traces to destroy.

But God's all-seeing eye was watching,
   To bring to light this fearful crime,
And now the murderer pale and trembling,
   Awaits for trial the appointed time.
If the jury find him guilty,
   To eternity he'll soon be hurled,
To meet his mutilated victims,
   Face to face in another world.

H P. SUCH, Machine Printer and Publisher, 177, Union Street, Borough, S.E.

In Memory of

JOSEPH WOOD.

AGED 58 YEARS,

AND HIS SON

JOSEPH THOMPSON,

AGED 9 YEARS,

Who were brutally Murdered by Robert Charter,
at Cropton-lane Farm, near Pickering, May 17th, 1872.

No one to help them—no one to save,
No one but Heaven to point out their grave,
The poor man and boy who had done him no harm,
Were murdered by Charter, at Cropton-lane Farm.

A poem and funeral card in memory of Joseph Wood, aged 58 and his son Joseph Thompson, aged 9 who were brutally murdered by Robert Charter at Cropton Lane Farm, near Pickering on 17 May 1872.

Chapter 1

The Early Days

Murder is not as commonplace as people often imagine. Today, the media, whether newspaper or television, present an impression of murders occurring every day. In olden times such archives may not have existed to record the event so readily as now. Indeed, in the earliest period records probably never probably existed at all, but some brief memorandum may often remain to leave a tantalising trace of a grisly deed. Because of this, the deed often lives on longer than the names of the victim and assailant. Time may dim the memory, but the idea of unlawfully taking a human life is so abhorrent to most people that for centuries afterwards, locals recount the tale until it often becomes folklore.

Along the East Coast such tantalising fragments include perhaps the earliest murder mystery of this geographical area. Roman signal stations stretch out along the shore and cliff all down the coast of Yorkshire, established to give warning and defence against attack from sea raids by Norse and Teutonic pirates.

So long ago as the year 1817, George Young, a cleric and antiquarian in Whitby, conjectured that there was probably a fort on Whitby East Cliff to defend the harbour, another at Scarborough, one near Filey Brig, and one on Flamborough Head (Figure 1).[1]

Figure 1. *The cliffs at Flamborough from which the Romans kept watch for pirates and raiders.*

However, it was not until 1912 that actual proof of these hit-and-run raids by marauding seafarers was obtained, when a late-Roman fort was unearthed at Huntcliff near Saltburn, by Mr William Hornby and Mr R Stanton.

The fort was a small look-out station, which the report in the *Journal of Roman Studies*[2] says, 'had a short life and untimely end'. It appears to have been taken by assault and burnt, the luckless inhabitants killed and thrown into a small well which was discovered within the confines of the fort. In this well were found many human bones, including fourteen skulls, all but four considerably damaged.

In the very interesting description published in the previously mentioned publication, the author of the article states:

> *It is fairly certain that in the later Roman period the north-east coast of Britain was vexed by pirates from across the seas, Saxons, Angles and the like. To such pirates the splendid stretch of sands between Huntcliff and the mouth of the Tees offered useful beaching ground. Under Huntcliff there is a landing place now called 'Penny Hole'; which is available in the stormiest weather, and is still used by fishers in sudden gales. The early pirate may well have known of this landing place and employed it. The Romans, in order to check him, planted an outlook post from which warning signals by beacon, could be passed both inland and up and down the coast.*

After the excavation at Huntcliff had been completed, the archaeologists moved down the coast eventually reaching Kettleness, and there, in the Goldsborough Pasture on a lofty eminence at 425 feet above sea level, at a distance of a half mile from the sea, a second signal station was unearthed.

The Goldsborough signal station was discovered and excavated by Messrs William Hornby and J D Laverick between 1918 and 1923. A full report with many illustrations was published in 1932 in the *Archaeological Journal*, Vol. LXXXIX.[3]

Although the Goldsborough encampment did not yield as many bones as that at Huntcliff, one sensational discovery was made in the south-east corner of the station (Figure 2).

> *A short, thick-set man had fallen across the smouldering fire of an open hearth, probably after having been stabbed in the back. His skeleton lay face downwards, the left hand, on which was a bronze ring, behind the back, the right touching the south wall. Another skeleton, that of a taller man, also lay face down, near the feet of the*

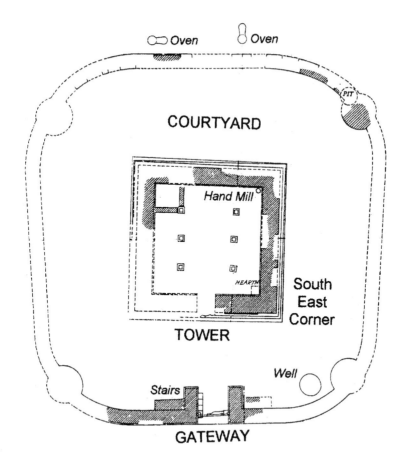

Figure 2. *Plan of the Roman Signal Station at Goldsborough (excluding surround ditch) based on a drawing in the* Archaelogical Journal, *Vol. LXXXIX.*

first, his head pointing south-west. Beneath him was the skeleton of a large and powerful dog, its head against the man's throat, its paws across his shoulders - surely a grim record of a desperate drama, perhaps with the dog as one of the defenders and his victim an intruder. Near the feet of the second skeleton were two silver coins of Eugenius and Honorius.

Nothing remains today of the fort at Kettleness. Time and erosion has removed all traces of the tragedy enacted there. No memorial exists to mark the event. However, on the North York Moors behind the coastal plain, is a reminder of one of the earliest recorded murders in Yorkshire. In AD 626 a ghastly crime was committed against none other than a member of royalty, which tragically led to the death of an innocent man.

Figure 3. *Lilla Cross, North Yorkshire Moors.*

Figure 4. *Skipsea Castle, showing the motte in the distance surrounded by a defensive ditch in the foreground.*

In that year, an assassination was plotted against Edwin, King of Northumbria (d.633) in a battle for control of his vast kingdom that stretched from the river Humber up to the borders of Scotland and which encompassed the North York Moors. The King of the West Saxons intent on having this land sent an assassin to kill Edwin as he journeyed across Fylingdales Moor. The assassin struck with a poisoned sword, but Edwin's devoted man-servant, a Christian named Lilla, sprang between the assassin and King Edwin. Lilla took the death-blow and died as a result of his action.

So impressed was Edwin that he became a Christian and later built a fine stone church at York which in time became York Minster. Meanwhile, to honour the valour of Lilla, a stone cross was erected on the moor where he fell and that is now called Lilla Cross (Figure 3). It stands as a landmark some 959 feet above sea level upon Lilla Howe, almost in the shadow of RAF Fylingdales Early Warning Station and forms part of a network of crosses that serve as a guide to those who trek across the heights from Robin Hood's Bay to remote moorland communities.

Skipsea is some seven miles south of Bridlington and several miles east of the rolling hills of the Wolds. It is one of several Holderness villages which have, throughout their history, been threatened by the relentless North Sea. Quite literally, the sea comes closer with each passing year. Today, the waves are less than a mile from the village.

In the time of William the Conqueror, Skipsea was a place of considerable importance but it is now a quiet village which visitors usually pass through *en route* to either Bridlington or Hornsea. However, some do make the effort to stay locally and to explore the coastline hereabouts. There are some interesting old cottages here, particularly those built of pebbles from the beach. Such cottages are a direct contrast to the many chalk-built houses that feature along this coast. To the west of the thirteenth century pebble-built church which was restored in 1866, there are some large earthworks which serve as a reminder of Skipsea's former stature (Figure 4).

One, known as Albemarle Hill, is probably a natural mound but was the site of an important castle. The man who erected the castle was named Drogo de Beurere or Brevere, who was described in the *Chronicle of Meaux Abbey* as a Flemish adventurer. He fought alongside William the Conqueror at the Battle of Hastings in 1066 and was honoured by being allowed to marry one of the king's nieces. His greatest honour, however, was to be granted the Seignory of Holderness by King William I (1027-87).

It was in this manner then, that Drogo became the Lord of

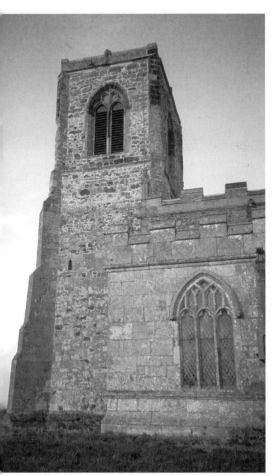

Figure 5. *The west tower of Skipsea church which stands near to Skipsea Castle.*

Holderness, a vast tract of land which spreads along the coastline. Drogo settled on Skipsea for his home and built his castle here. He selected the hilltop site to the west of the present church where it is suggested that there was possibly a stronghold before the time of Drogo (Figure 5). He erected a fine motte and bailey castle of wood, with a wooden draw-bridge over the moat. It was to this place, a splendid building in its day, that Drogo de Brevere brought his new bride.

But sadly tragedy came to the Lady of Holderness; she was killed by her husband in mysterious circumstances. History does not acquaint us by what means she met her end, nor does it enlighten us as to whether her death was an accident or murder. We do not know the manner of her demise either. Was she stabbed, beaten, drowned or poisoned? The only note of her end occurs in a contemporary record which says she was killed *omine infausto*.[4] Locals believed that she was poisoned by Drogo who blamed her for his change of fortune after he moved to Skipsea, and somehow coming to believe that she was a sorceress. It was whispered that he persuaded her to drink from a chalice laced with poison and secretly buried her body near the castle.

Afterwards, however, possibly overcome with guilt, Drogo also became fearful of the king's reaction and decided to conceal the news of her death from him. But such a state of affairs could not persist. In time the servants became suspicious about the sudden disappearance of their mistress. They began to discuss it among themselves and then the villagers got to hear about their fears. Drogo hurried to meet William and asked to borrow money, giving for his reason the lie that he wanted to return temporarily to Flanders and take his wife with him. He said she was homesick and would benefit from a short period in her homeland. It appears King William believed the story and gave the necessary loan to him. Drogo lost no time in escaping overseas, leaving his dead wife buried in Skipsea.

With Drogo away, the servants began to search for their Lady and soon discovered her lifeless corpse. They raised the alarm; the Conqueror was notified with all possible speed and was furious at the murder and the deception. He sent his constables to arrest Drogo. They searched all his known haunts and possible escape routes. But it was too late. Drogo had fled and was never seen again.

His vast lands in Holderness were confiscated and presented to a new lord called Odo, by William. He was also the Lord of Albemarle, a son of the Count of Champagne and husband of another of the Conqueror's nieces named Adeliza. Odo, however, did not appreciate his new gift - he complained to the King that the land was barren, except for oats, and so William added to his gift by giving Odo Bytham, in Lincolnshire, so that he could bring up his son on wheaten bread. The Seignory of Holderness continued in the hands of the House of Albemarle until the reign of King Edward I (1272-1307) when it reverted to the Crown, due to the lack of male heirs in the family. The castle, however, seems to have disappeared before this time. One of the earls of Albemarle, William de Fortibus, rebelled against King Henry III (1216-72) and the king's response was simple. In the year 1220, he ordered that the castle be raised to the ground.

Another possible early murder mystery centres on a number of human skeletons unearthed in November 1894. These were discovered during the progress of work upon the site of the Franciscan Schools, in Scarborough, then in the course of erection.[5] A Franciscan monastery had stood on the spot some three or four centuries earlier. Among the skeletons found, was one that had, what was evidently a piece of rope in the form of a noose encircling the vertebrae of the neck.

Was this a case of a medieval monk entering into a pact with his fellow brothers at a time of persecution to save them all from possible inhumane torture? Or a case of simple multiple murder, with the perpetrator in a fit of remorse taking his own life by hanging? Possibly we shall never know the truth of it.

Chapter 2

The Murdered Hermit of Eskdale –
Sir Richard de Veron (*d.*1160)

Perhaps the most famous of all the earliest murders to occur in the Whitby area, concerns the murdered hermit of Eskdale. Eskdale forms part of the parish of Eskdale-cum-Ugglebarnby, but is more locally and nationally identified as the village of Sleights (Figure 6), which lays some three miles outside the seaport of Whitby, just under the lee of the Yorkshire moors and before the road rises out of the valley of the river Esk up that famous steep ascent known as Blue Bank. Here, in the time just after the Norman conquest, when the land in this parish was covered almost entirely in woods, took place a most foul deed that gave rise to a most curious ceremony which takes place on the morning of the eve of Ascension Day every year in the sands of the harbour of Whitby at low tide.

Sir Richard de Veron was a distinguished knight of the North Riding, who held a considerable estate by knight's service of the De Brus family in Cleveland. He was one of the heroes of the Battle of the Standard, in 1138, and who went forth at the behest of

Figure 6. *Sleights village, three miles from Whitby.*

Archbishop Thurstan to oppose the invasion of King David of Scotland; and who signally defeated the monarch. A few years after, he joined the forces of the Empress Maud, whose pretensions to the throne of England he considered to be more legitimate than those of King Stephen. He fought on her side at Lincoln, in 1141, when the King was defeated and taken prisoner, continuing to uphold her cause until Maud was compelled to retire from England. After this conflict was brought to an end, and the adherents of the Empress generally declined to take sevice under a monarch who they deemed a usurper, and by whom they were looked upon in turn by the king with suspicion, De Veron sheathed his sword and retired to his family and home in Cleveland. He had a wife, whom he loved dearly, and two children, a boy – his heir, and a sweet little daughter for whom he entertained the most tender affection. Indeed, although he delighted in the clash of arms and the exciting revelry of war, he was never so truly happy as when in the midst of his family.

Months passed by. Sir Richard was content and the horrors of the war between Empress Maud and King Stephen began to fade. Then one morning news was brought that a case of plague had occurred in the village, causing, as it always did, great consternation not only among the villagers but in the knight's mansion, which stood half a mile away. It was hoped that it was to be an isolated case, but within a week another case was reported, and another in rapid succession, after which it spread with fearful speed, until half the population succumbed to it, and were hastily buried without the usual funeral rites. In a month the disease appeared to be dying out, the deaths became fewer and fewer day by day, and it was fondly hoped that the terrible affliction was passing away, but it was not until three-quarters of the people had fallen victim to its pestilential fury that it finally ended.

Sir Richard took all rude remedial measures as were then known to prevent the spread of the infection within his own household. However, his duties took him into the village and although he had adopted as many of the measures as were practical and endeavoured to take precautions against coming into too close contact with the infected, he was at last stricken down. Taking to a separate set of apartments, he entreated his wife and family to remain away. He gave positive orders that he should be left alone, and if it was God's will that he should die, he declared his resolution that he should die alone. But she, true wife as she was, heeded not the risk to her own life, so long as she could afford comfort and spiritual consolation to her beloved husband in what might very possibly be his last few moments on earth. Gentle reproaches by Sir Richard were useless, and in his sickness, too weak to fight further, he submitted to her nursing. Happily, during the night the malady passed its crisis, and his strong, generally healthy constitution enabled him to battle successfully with the disease, and he gradually became convalescent.

With his return to full health, happiness again seemed to dawn over the household of this knight, but it was not destined to last long. The faithful wife, who had watched so tenderly over his sick bed, regardless of the risk she ran, maintained her own health so long as her services were needed, and now, when her husband was restored to health, the terrible plague spot made its appearance on her, and so rapidly did the disease develop itself, that, within twenty-four hours, she fell victim to its remorseless energy and passed away. Yet not content, the disease took hold of his two children, and in another twenty-four hours they were both carried off, leaving Sir Richard de Veron bereft of his entire family, and sunk in the depths of desolation and despair.

His grief was utter and all consuming, and for months he remained in his silent and cheerless home in a state of profound apathy, taking no interest in the vocations devolving upon him as the lord of an extensive estate. In time the only person whom he admitted as a visitor, beside those who came on imperative business matters, was Father Anselm, a pious and devout man and priest of the village church. It was in his company only, and in listening to his spiritual conversation, that he felt any relief from the grief that oppressed him, and gradually, after many interviews, he began to look upon his affliction as a providential dispensation, intended for some wise purpose. Gradually too, he became more weaned from earthly and secular thoughts and began to experience an attraction to the cloister. One day he mentioned this to his spiritual adviser, and Father Anselm warmly applauded the feeling, urging that such self-devotion would be most acceptable to God, and saying that it was only in religious meditation and prayer that he would find true consolation. The holy father, however, was perhaps not altogether single-mined in fostering the idea of assuming the cowl, for he was a true Churchman, considering that the promotion of the temporal aggrandisement of the Church was an essential part of the duty of a Christian, a sentiment then universally prevalent. He knew that Sir Richard was the owner of broad acres, and that now he had no heir to inherit them, and he often made delicate and incidental allusions to the fact, which in due course seemed to produce an impression on the mind of the knight. At last an opportunity offered itself of

Whitby Abbey and Church About 1300

Figure 7. *Whitby Abbey and church about the year 1300.*

speaking more openly on the subject. In response, Sir Richard consented to give some thought to Father Anselm's words and agreed within a week he would make a decision on whether to make the holy Church of Christ his heir.

At the week end, when they met again, Sir Richard opened the subject by saying,

> *Venerable Father, I have since our last meeting given deep consideration to your counsels, and have come to the resolution of doing as you advise me. I have determined on assuming the monkish habit; spending the remainder of my life in pious communion with some holy brotherhood; and on resigning my possessions into the hands of the Church of God.*

After this speech, the two sat to consider which would be the best religious house for the good knight to enter. Sir Richard at first considered becoming a canon of the Augustinian house recently founded by his feudal lord, Robert de Brus, at Guisborough. However, Father Anselm countered with the opinion that the Augustinian house at Guisborough was not so strict in discipline as other monastic houses and very fairly endowed with riches. He proposed the Benedictine order, and in particular, the abbey at Whitby, now refounded but lacking an endowment for the due maintenance of its superior dignity (Figure 7).

Let me advise you, therefore, to cast in your lot with these Benedictines, and win the approval of God by bestowing your wealth in his service, where it is much needed.

Sir Richard assented to this suggestion, caused a deed of gift to be drawn up, in which he conveyed his lands to the Abbot and convent of Whitby, and entered the house as a novice. In due time, at the expiration of his novitiate, was admitted to the cloister as a monk, taking a new name.

Brother Jerome (to use his monastic appellation) soon attracted notice by the fervour of his piety, his asceticism, and a strict and sincere observance of the conventual rules; as well as by his humility and obedience to the ordinances of his superiors. After he had been in the house for a few years, the Prior sickened and died; and, at a meeting of the chapter to elect his successor, Brother Jerome was suggested as the most fitting; but he resolutely declined, preferring to be the servant of the brotherhood than to hold any superior office. It was also at this time, while in the course of his meditations on what course of action to take regarding the offer of the chapter, that he was wont to examine his past life, and come to grieve over his career as a soldier. The more he thought of these past phases of his life, the more intense became his self-reproaches and the compunction excited by a sense of guilt and sin. He sought by mortification and maceration of the flesh to make atonement for these blood-stained deeds, but despite these self-inflicted punishments, he was not able to find rest for his soul.

At length he unburdened himself to the Abbot, an old, wise, and experienced Christian, who counselled him not to put aside the cowl and return to earthly pleasures as was the first thought of Brother Jerome, deeming his life now worthless, but to consider withdrawing himself entirely from communion with his fellow-creatures, even from the Holy Brotherhood of Whitby, and devote the remainder of his existence to solitary meditation and prayer altogether apart from the world. Brother Jerome agreed.

Connected with the abbey of Whitby there was, in a solitary place within the forest that fringed the banks of the river Esk, a chapel where the monks were wont to retire at certain seasons for the purpose of devotion and meditation away from the bustle and distractions inevitable in a large community (Figure 8). Here, in close proximity to this chapel, Brother Jerome built for himself a wooden shelter in which to pass his remaining years as a hermit. Secluded from society, he lived on wild fruit and roots, quenching his

Figure 8. *Eskdale Chapel shortly after closure in the eighteenth century.*

thirst from the brook which trickled past, and spending his days and nights in prayer, flagellation, and abstinence.

At this date there was resident in the neighbourhood of Whitby two landed proprietors, Ralph de Percy, lord of Sneaton, and William de Brus, lord of Ugglebarnby, who were great lovers of hunting and other field sports, and near them lived a member of the Allatson family, a gentleman and freeholder. The three were boon companions, and constantly met in the pursuit of country sports, and entertained each other in their respective houses for the purpose of carousing together. One night when they were thus assembled together they arranged to hunt boar in the forest of Eskdale on the following day, which was the sixteen of October, in the fifth year of the reign of King Henry II (1157).

Next day, at the appointed hour the three did meet and garbed in their hunting attire, with boar-staves in their hands, and accompanied by a pack of boar-hounds, yelping and barking, and as eager for the sport as their masters, set out into the forest to hunt the wild boar. Soon a great boar was started, which plunged into the recesses of the woods, followed by the hounds in full cry, and by the hunters, shouting to encourage them. Onward they all rushed, the maddened wild boar, the dogs in hot pursuit, and the three with blood-lust, intent on having the beast. Eventually, the boar being very sore and very hotly pursued, and dead run, took in at the chapel door of the hermit Brother Jerome, and there died. At this point the hermit shut the hounds out of the chapel and kept himself within at his meditations, the hounds standing at bay without.

Soon after, the gentlemen came upon the hounds baying round the hermitage door which sat firmly shut. The three called out to the hermit Brother Jerome, who opened the chapel door, whereon they espied the boar within, dead. In great fury at the spoiled sport, they did in anger most violently and cruelly, run at the hermit with their boar-staves and injured him severely.

After the attack, and suddenly calmed by the result of their actions the three fearful of the consequences of their crime, fled to Scarborough, and took sanctuary in the church. But the Abbot of Whitby, who was a friend of the King, was authorised to take them out, 'whereby they came in danger of the law, and not to be privileged, but likely to have the severity of the law, which was death.'

Meanwhile, the hermit, who had been brought to Whitby Abbey, lay at the point of death when the prisoners where brought thither; and hearing of their arrival, he besought the abbot that they might be brought into his presence. When they made their appearance, he said to them, 'I am sure to die of these wounds you gave me.' 'Yes,' said the abbot, 'And they in turn shall die for their crime.' 'Not so,' continued the dying man, 'for I will freely forgive them my death if they will be content to be enjoined this penance for the safeguard of their souls.' 'Enjoin what penance you will,' replied the culprits, 'so that our lives may be spared.'

Then spoke the dying hermit -

You and yours shall hold your lands of the Abbot of Whitby and his successors in this manner. That upon Ascension Eve, you, or some of you, shall come to the woods of Stray-heads, which is in Eskdale, the same day at sunrising, and there shall the abbot's officer blow his horn, to the intent that you may know how to find him; and he shall deliver unto you, William de Brus, ten stakes, eleven strutstowers, and eleven yethers, to be cut by you, or some of you, with a knife of one penny price; and you, Ralph de Percy, shall take twenty and one of each sort, to be cut in the same manner; and you, Allatson, shall take nine of each sort to be cut aforesaid, and to be taken on your backs and carried to the town of Whitby, and to be there before nine of the clock the same day before mentioned. If at the same hour of nine of the clock it be full sea, your labour or service shall cease; but if it be not full sea, each of you shall set your stakes at the brim and so yether them, on each side of your yethers, and so stake on each side with your strowers, that they may stand three tides, without removing by the force thereof. Each of you shall make and execute the said service at that very hour, every year, except it shall be full sea at that hour; but when it shall so fall out, this service shall cease... You shall faithfully do this, in remembrance that you did most cruelly slay me; and that you may the better call to God for mercy, repent unfeignedly for your sins, and do good works. The officer of Eskdale-side shall blow - 'Out on you! Out on you! Out on you!' for this heinous crime. If you, or your successors, shall refuse this service, so long as it shall not be full sea, at the aforesaid hour, you, or yours, shall forfeit your lands to the Abbot of Whitby, or his successors. This I entreat, and earnestly beg that you may have lives and goods preserved for this service; and I request of you to promise, by your parts in Heaven, that it shall be done by you and your successors as it is aforesaid requested.

And the abbot said, 'I grant all that you have spoken, and I will confirm it by the faith of an honest man.' Then the hermit said, 'My soul longeth for the Lord; and I do freely forgive these men my death, as Christ forgave the thief upon the cross.' Then in the presence of the abbot and the rest, he said these words - *In manas tuas, domine, commendo spiritum, meum, avinculis enim mortis redemisti me Domine veritatis. Amen* - and on completion, did yield up the ghost the eighth day of December, AD 1160.

In 1753, the service was rendered by the last of the Allatson family, the Lords of Sneaton and Ugglebarnby having, it is supposed, bought off their share of the penance. This Allatson held a piece of land valued at £10 a year, at Fylingdales, from which he brought five stakes, eight yethers, and six strutstowers, and whilst the bailiff of Mr Cholmley, then lord of the manor of Whitby, did on an antique bugle blow 'Out on you!' he did make a fence of them a little way into the shallow of the river. Burton, writing in 1757, adds, 'This little farm is now out of the Allatson family, but the present owner performed the service last Ascension Eve, AD 1756.'

It is said that the 'Horngarth' or 'Penny Hedge' as the fence is now called, was constructed on the East Side of the river Esk for the purposes of keeping cattle from straying into the landing places. At this date, the beach sloped down from the houses to the waters edge and beasts freely roamed along the shore and were wont to impede

Figure 9. *Planting the Penny Hedge ceremony in 1907.*

those landing goods. Charlton, in his *History of Whitby* states that the making of the horngarth is of a much older date than that indicated by the tale of the murdered hermit.[6]

Today the ceremony is still performed, and has been continually enacted since the eighteenth century (Figure 9), with only a short break in modern times during the war years and in most recent years in 1981 when the tide was too high and prevented the hedge being planted. In the millennium year 2000, the construction of the hedge was undertaken by the Bailiff of the Manor of Fyling and Mr Tim Osborne, Goathland Hunt Secretary, watched by a good size crowd of sightseers on Wednesday, 31 May, and at the end of October of the same year, I noticed as I passed the spot marked with a stone and plaque beside the road along Church Street, that the Penny Hedge still stood against the tide.[7]

Chapter 3

The Fight for Hornsea Fishery
~1260 ~

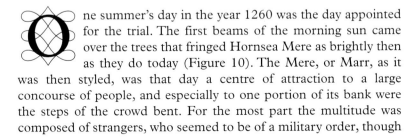ne summer's day in the year 1260 was the day appointed for the trial. The first beams of the morning sun came over the trees that fringed Hornsea Mere as brightly then as they do today (Figure 10). The Mere, or Marr, as it was then styled, was that day a centre of attraction to a large concourse of people, and especially to one portion of its bank were the steps of the crowd bent. For the most part the multitude was composed of strangers, who seemed to be of a military order, though

Figure 10. *Hornsea Mere looking toward Hornsea village showing the old windmill in the distance.*

there was a goodly number of farm-servants and others of the neighbouring manors. Whatever their station or appearance, however, one subject was the theme or conversation which bound them, and that was the combat which was to be fought that day by the side of the picturesque little lake. The lake itself, or rather the right to fish therein, was the object of the fight. The Abbot of Meaux claimed the right of taking the fish in the southern part of the waters, while the Abbot of St Mary's Abbey, in York, asserted that the right was his alone. Now at a time when fast days could only be made feast days by a plentiful supply of fish, such a privilege was one not to be lightly forgone; so each worthy monk held out for the coveted prescription of his respective house. They had first tried the matter by means of parchment and pen without settling the vexed question. At length, therefore, it had been decided to try the virtue of the sword and battle-hammer, by strength of arms and skill of eye, which the vain superstition of the age imagined would be unerringly guide by Heaven in the cause of right - in short, a trial by combat.

All was gaiety and mirth; everyone was too much accustomed to arms to think this a serious matter. Even the twelve champions, six for each of the abbots, grimly joked on the sacerdotal character of their masters as they donned their barrel-shaped helmets, and put right the last buckle of their padded leather armour, or ringed mail, and adjusted the small caps or plates which covered their joints. Upon palfreys of becoming docility, were mounted the rival abbots, each surrounded by no mean retinue of well-armed dependants. There stood, or rode slowly about the place, the knight who had been appointed Marshall, and with his heralds kept order, appointing places of vantage to strangers to view the fight. He also took notice that none interfered with the boundary stakes; these had been fixed the previous day by a mounted horseman swimming his steed across the Mere to decide what was the exact limit of right to be exercised by the victorious abbot, whichever he might happen to be.

At last all was ready. In a wide ring the two groups of warriors stood facing each other awaiting the signal to begin the affray. Each knight, each champion, was fully armed in the panoply of their day, and that was, as nearly as may be said, in the manner of the average cross-legged crusaders upon the tombs in our homeland churches. Each man had a shield, a pointless sword, and either a pointed hammer, or a flail-like mace. The six champions of Meaux (the plaintiffs) had surcoats embroidered with a cross, with birds in the angles; the others had upon their surcoats what may have been a simple large cross.

The herald's trumpet sound. The Marshall gave the signal. The combat commenced, and every spectator thrust his chin eagerly over the shoulder of the one in front, and with beating pulse felt all the high ecstatic pleasure of the field echoed in his breast.

The two little forces rush swiftly at each other like two herds of deer, and in a second are in the heat of strike. They meet; blows are delivered and parried - till down with a crash, falls great Hubert, the best champion of the Yorkists. He is up again, - no, Brian of Meaux has struck his uplifted shield, once, twice, thrice, till his arm is bent, and he is prostrate once more. Forward rush two others of the Yorkist camp, bestride his struggling figure, and beat back his assailants, and young Brian, with a plate picked off his armour by Hubert's martel-de-fer, is bleeding at the knee. Hubert rises, and the combatants stand back to draw breath, only to rush together again a little to the right, where Gilbert and ban, both of the Meaux side, are attacking John of the Ouse, who retreats as best he may. Once again all the glittering swords are scintillating in one confused anvil-striking; lunge and parry, feint and thrust, succeed each other fast and thick, so that the eye cannot see quickly enough to note all the feats of skill and strength displayed. The burly Hubert throws his shield at the head of one opponent, felling him to the ground senseless, while William of Atwick, not to be outdone, hurls his shield spinning to the edge of the killing ground, the lists, and with his mace - a heavy ball studded with spikes swinging by a chain from a short wooden staff - rushes like a demon clean through the York champions. Two fall, with bruised mail and bleeding limbs, before he is seized in the arms of John of the Ouse, and cast headlong at the feet of his fellow knights. Panting and bleeding the sixes face each other once more when the trumpet sounds, and a brief interval is allowed for rest and the dressing of wounds.

Noon goes passed in more wary fight and longer intervals of rest. The noon gone by, long shadows steal slowly and silently across the lists. The combatants renew themselves at each fresh attack. Each incident of the morning fight is once more played out, yet now the warriors stand bruised and battered, and red with blood where not washed with the streams from perspiring brows, and the blows by this hour want some of the vigour of the early day.

The vesper bell of Nunkeeling Church is heard within a pause (Figure 11). It seems now that the champions of sword are as well-matched as those of the pen had been; when at the sound, feeling the decisive hour at hand, the Yorkists throw all their energy into one final effort of arms. Brian is hurled by a supreme effort of

Figure 11. *The church at Nunkeeling.*

Hubert clear of the lists, and so is out of the fight by the laws of
combat. At odds, the remaining five of Meaux are now unable to
stem the torrent of blows that come beating and rattling down about
their ears. Shields already battered are broken, bruised arms are
beaten powerless, and two more of the Meaux champions lie in
defeat from grievous wounds, of which one of them afterwards is to
die. The other three, after brief struggle, are too thrown down, and
the knights of York have won! The right to fish is theirs. And so by
right of might the monks of Meaux lost forever the fish in Hornsea
Mere, and their abbey table has to be supplied from other waters
elsewhere.

Chapter 4

The Martyr of Egton Bridge –
Father Nicholas Postgate (1597-1679)

One of the most interesting and arresting personalities of the Whitby district in the latter half of the seventeenth century, was the Venerable Nicholas Postgate, DD, who laid down his life for his faith at York on 7 August 1679, at the patriarchal age of eighty-two. Dragged on a wooden sledge through the city streets from York Castle, he was to suffer a most vicious death at Knavesmire, then known as Tyburn, and the place of execution. Here he was hung by the neck, then while still alive his entrails were cut out – drawn – and after death his body was cut up – quartered. Further indignities included the removal of the top joint of the forefinger, since this is where he held the Sacred Host during Mass. And in the gruesome manner of the time, relics such as his dismembered hands, strands of hair, scraps of clothing stained with his blood, the hangman's rope, and other items were sold off for souvenirs.

Nicholas Postgate was born at Kirkdale House, Egton, during the height of the persecution against Roman Catholics in the reign of Queen Elizabeth I. A writer in 1838 described the house in which he was born as standing near Egton Bridge and being 'little better than a cattle shed' (Figure 12). Even when new and the family lived there it must have been only a poor cottage in spite of its grand title it was situated just below the present massive Catholic Church of St Hedda beside the bridge that spans the river Esk. Today nothing remains of the ruins of the tiny cottage and it is probable that it was totally destroyed during the awful flood of 1930.

Figure 12. *Detail from an original watercolour painting showing Egton Bridge c.1800; Father Postgate's cottage is shown near the bridge.*

In spite of his fame within the community and among the Catholic faith, very little is known of his early life. It appears he was the youngest of three sons born to James and Margaret Postgate, his brothers being named Matthew and William. His father was a farmer or farm worker, perhaps on the estate, who was also born at Kirkdale House, and died young. In the year 1604 his widowed mother was branded a 'Recusant' – a Catholic who refused to conform to the established religion. Others of the family were also likewise branded, and a note in the parish records reads,

Jane Postgate doth keep in her house William Postgate, her father, a Recusant, who teacheth children, and also Marmaduke Petch and Jane Smallwood, Recusants. [8]

Among the childhood stories of Nicholas Postgate is one which suggests that, in January 1616, he was fined ten shillings at Helmsley Quarter Sessions for being a member of a band of strolling players or minstrels who were found begging. They were performing music and plays that were critical of the Protestant religion and the authorities tried to prevent this. This Nicholas Postgate was then described as a 'thirteen year old farm labourer from Egton'. It is not certain, however, whether this Nicholas is the same, as our Nicholas Postgate would probably have been a few years older, assuming his date of birth is reasonably correct.

In 1621, however, what is certain, is that he was sent abroad to the famous Catholic College at Douay, in France to continue his education and in time to become a Catholic priest. Training for the Catholic priesthood was illegal in England at that time, and it was the custom in those days for the students to take another name, since it was a penal offence for Catholics to be educated abroad, and, if known by their proper names, they might bring trouble on their parents at home. At College, Nicholas Postgate called himself Whitmore or Whitemore, perhaps a witty reference to the fact that his home was in 'Blackmoor', as this area of the North York Moors around Egton Bridge was then known. Later, when engaged in mission work, he passed by the name of Watson, the name of his maternal grandfather.

Nicholas was rather older than the average student, but he worked hard and took an active part in the running of the College. On 23 October 1627, there is a note to say he was the Sacristan, during which time he gave good service. Finally, on 20 March in the following year he was ordained. He was now Father Postgate, the name by which he is more commonly known.

Figure 13. *Abbey House, Whitby, beside the ruins of Whitby Abbey.*

On 29 June 1630, Father Nicholas Postgate returned to England. His task was to join the English Mission, designed to revive the Catholic faith which had suffered so much during the Reformation and at the hands of the Protestant persecutors.

Many martyrs had been executed, many of whom came from the North-East, but this only strengthened his resolve to battle for his beliefs. It is possible that Father Postgate landed at Whitby; there were strong links between the North Riding of Yorkshire and the College at Douay, and many priests secretly returning to England, had landed at this northern seaport.

Here at Whitby, were many adherents to the faith and supporters of Catholicism, and a number of 'safe houses' or 'clearing houses' existed wherein priests could sleep and find food until they could travel in safety to their new livings. Lady Catherine Scrope, widow of Lord Scrope, of Bolton, kept Abbey House at Whitby, beside the ruins of the great Benedictine Abbey and therein sheltered priests (Figure 13). Bagdale Old Hall and Ugthorpe Hall were other houses among many in the district which gave shelter and employment to Catholic priests during the days of persecution. Others also included Grosmont Priory, Upsall Castle near Thirsk, Bridge-holme Green at Egton Bridge, and a house in the Shambles at York run by Margaret Clitherow, herself martyred and later raised to sainthood.

At Ugthorpe Hall (Figure 14), which at that time was the seat of the Radcliffe family, Catholics who suffered much for their faith, there was an outbuilding near to the house which was used as a cow byre, in which there was a curious 'Priest Hole' contrived in a chimney. Another barn or byre on the right-hand side as you faced the front entrance of Ugthorpe Hall, was once a Catholic Chapel, though there was little enough to show of its proper use.

Father Postgate firstly became chaplain to Sir William and Lady Hungate, at Saxton Hall near Tadcaster. After which for the next thirty years, he served as chaplain to families resident at several manor houses throughout Yorkshire. He was at Hazlewood Castle, in the West Riding, now a hotel, where he administered to the religious needs of the Vavasours, a most distinguished Catholic family. Nicholas Postgate also served 'old Lady Dunbar' at Burton Constable in East Yorkshire; at Everingham with a junior branch of the Dunbar family; at Kilvington Castle, near Thirsk in the North Riding with the Meynell family and at Kilvington Hall with the Saltmarsh family. For a priest, chaplaincy to the landed gentry provided some measure of safety and comfort, even if at times priests were treated more like servants than educated spiritual advisors and for awhile Father Postgate revelled in a life of reasonable comfort and security. However, from the early part of 1660 he chose a different direction in life and for his chief abode Father Postgate lived in a small thatched cottage at Ugthorpe, two miles from Mulgrave Castle,

Figure 14. *Ugthorpe Hall, front elevation.*

in the midst of wild moorland. Here he lived as a poor man among the poor, conforming in dress, diet and lodging to the flock that he zealously tended. Today, the site of the cottage of Father Postgate is called The Hermitage, and parts of its walls are incorporated into the farm buildings that stand upon its foundations.

From this lonely spot, Father Postgate began to concentrate on missionary work restoring the Catholic faith in and around the moorland villages of Egton,

Figure 15. *A portrait of Father Postgate painted on wood and now in the museum at Whitby.* Whitby Museum

Grosmont, Glaisdale, Ugthorpe, Sleights and Whitby. Inevitably, however, his travels extended much further. He went over the moors to Guisborough in the North-East, and to the Pickering and Helmsley areas in the southern part of the North Riding. During his travels it is recorded that he often travelled in the disguise of a pedlar or a jobbing gardener, an employment he enjoyed immensely we are told. His life was always at risk and there was constant danger from local informers and pursuivants.

He became a familiar figure around the countryside, dressed in a rough brown habit in the manner of a monk (Figure 15). In wet weather over this he wore a white button-up cape of canvas material and he usually employed a long staff as an aid to walking. In stature he was generally thought of as a small wiry man whose rugged existence had removed any excess weight from his frame. He wore a long full beard that acted as a protection to his throat as he suffered from a recurring throat infection. White hair and blues eyes set in a rather bland pale face completed his description. It is said that he was deep thinking and highly intelligent, with an interest in music and literature as well as horticulture. He was very proper in everything he did, and could be described as serious-minded, although he did possess a gentle sense of humour and an unquenchable spirit of cheerfulness.

As a travelling priest, Father Postgate would carry items for use during Mass. A collapsible chalice of French origin made in three

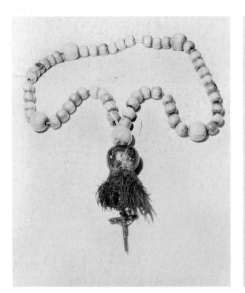 

Figure 16. *The rosary used by Father Postgate (left) and door of a portable tabernacle found in the Mass House (right).*

pieces which screwed together,[9] a small box with a secret locking system or cloth pyx for carrying the Sacred Host, small candles and altar condiments, missal, rosary and even a tiny altar stone made of slate (Figure 16). The items he carried would have been small enough to be concealed and not be readily identified as the artefacts of a Catholic priest. Equipped in this way he trekked around the wild desolate moors in all weathers.

He conducted Mass in the barns, outbuildings, lofts and quiet rooms of farmhouses and cottages, many of which still survive to this day. One of these dwellings is Mass House at Egton (Figure 17). It is situated on the right of Egton Bank, halfway between Egton Bridge and Egton. This sturdy stone-built cottage bears its name inscribed in a stone built into a south-facing wall. Here, Father Nicholas made use of Mass House as a chapel and issued notice of forthcoming services through a code that involved spreading white sheets on the hedgerows. As this was the custom used by country folk for drying their washing, it was the perfect method of secret communication. Again at Mass House as mentioned before elsewhere in other houses, there was secret rooms and an exit which led from the roof into the grounds outside. There are tales of Father Postgate making several flights by this route from sudden raids by pursuivants to gain freedom in the woods that then surrounded the cottage.

Figure 17. *The Mass House, Egton, dating from 1665 before restoration.*

It was not until 1830 that Mass House gave up its secret chapel, when a girl, cleaning the upper wall of the kitchen, fell through the plaster into a small dark loft measuring fifteen feet long by ten feet wide and five feet six inches high (Figure 18). A tunnel through the thatch provided a view of the outside and no doubt some of the congregation stood in the kitchen to hear Mass.

When the chapel was examined, it revealed an altar laid out for the celebration of Mass. There was a crucifix, a pair of candlesticks, a

Figure 18. *Model of the Mass House showing the hidden loft (right), now in St Hedda's Church. Egton Bridge.*

EGTON MASS HOUSE 1665

Figure 19. *St Hedda's Church, Egton Bridge.*

missal and even the priest's vestments. After more than 150 years, one of Father Postgate's secret loft chapels had been discovered and those relics, with many more, can be viewed in St Hedda's Church, at Egton Bridge (Figure 19). Finally, another surprise occurred in 1928 when the roof was being repaired. Twenty florins and six shillings from the reigns of Elizabeth I, Charles I and Charles II were unearthed in the thatch, probably a secret cache of money set aside for Father Postgate's use. These too, were placed on display in St Hedda's Church, but were later stolen in the mid-1970s.

For decades Father Postgate in a quiet and secretive manner undertook his mission to minister to the faithful and convert folk to Catholicism where appropriate. It seems he made friends with Protestant and Catholic alike; his pleasant and friendly manner, and his wholehearted devotion to God and his Church endeared him to all. There appeared no reason why he should not have continued his work without severe hindrance, especially in later life as by then the authorities were growing more relaxed in their attitudes toward Catholic priests. Indeed, by this period, they were unofficially allowed to practise their faith as long as it did not make waves. The old man, now aged eighty-one, would probably have gone to his grave in peace, had not the population suddenly been driven to frenzy by the discovery of the so-called 'Popish Plot'.

These falsehoods stimulated the persecuting zeal, not only of those misguided people who thought that they did God service by hunting Catholic priests to death, but also of every unprincipled ruffian who did not shrink from swearing away a man's life for a reward.[10]

On Sunday 8 December 1678, Father Postgate was called to baptise a child at the house of Matthew Lyth, a farmer who farmed Red Barns Farm in the valley of Littlebeck and following this perform Mass. While in the house he was apprehended by an exciseman named John Reeves, an implacable enemy of Catholics and a former servant of the murdered Sir Edmund Berry Godfrey, a highly respected but possibly corrupt Protestant Justice of the Peace of Westminster, in London, implicated in the 'Popish Plot' begun and fuelled by the Reverend Titus Oates, aged 28, and the Reverend Ezrael Tonge, aged 55. In his actions John Reeves was motivated by greed and hoped to gain the reward of twenty pounds offered to informants against Catholics. With him in his deed was an associate Henry Cockerill, a mariner from Whitby and William Cockerill who was the constable for Eskdaleside.

Father Postgate was carried off to Brompton, near Scarborough, where he was examined by Sir William Cayley, a magistrate, who listened to depositions sworn by Reeves and the two Cockerills, as well as that of a man named Robert Langdale. Father Postgate also made a statement, and endorsed some alterations to its wording by initialling the margin with 'NP' in large strong handwriting. After deliberations Sir William felt that there was sufficient evidence to present before a judge and therefore committed Father Nicholas Postgate to trial at York Assizes. Canon Raine, in his *York Castle Depositions*, printed the official account of the examination that took place:

John Reeves, his Majesty's surveyor or gauger for the town of Whitby, saith that upon the 7th instant, he was informed that Matthew Lith of Sleights, being at a wedding, should (sic) *speak these words: 'You talk of papists and protestants; but when the roast is ready, I know who shall have the first cut.'*

Upon notice whereof this informer thought himself obliged to search the said Matthew's house, which accordingly he did upon the 8th instant, supposing that some arms or ammunition might be found there, the said Matthew and his family being all Papists.

And he saith that though he was interrupted by the said Matthew,

> *he did find a supposed popish priest there* (called Postgate) *and also Popish books, relics, wafers, and several other things, all of which the said Postgate owned to be his. The said Postgate said that he was called Watson, but afterwards, being called by others the name of Postgate, he owned that to be his right name.*

From Brompton Father Nicholas was taken to York and incarcerated in York Castle to await trial. It seems that more evidence was called for because in March, other witnesses were summoned to Brompton to make statements to Sir William Cayley. These witnesses included Elizabeth Baxter, Elizabeth Wood and Richard Morrice, all of whom testified that Father Postgate had conducted Catholic services in their presence.

Father Postgate was imprisoned for almost four months before his trial which took place in the Guildhall, at York, in March 1679 during the Lent Assizes (Figure 20). He was not charged with any involvement in the fake Popish Plot that had been sadistically concocted by Titus Oates, but indicted for being a Catholic priest under the old penal statute passed almost a century earlier in 1585, which outlawed 'Jesuits, seminary priests and such like disobedient persons'. Contemporary accounts suggest that the judge did his best to have the prisoner acquitted, saying that there was no evidence of ordination, but the evidence of Baxter, Wood and Morrice swayed any of the jury's reservations. Father Nicholas Postgate was found guilty and sentenced to death. Later, Elizabeth Baxter who had testified against him, visited his cell in York Castle full of remorse and

Figure 20. *The Guildhall, York, from across the river Ouse.*

Figure 21. *The condemned cell, York Castle dungeon.*

seeking his forgiveness (Figure 21). This Father Postgate readily gave and even provided her with money to pay her way back home.

A further four months passed by before his execution. During this period Father Postgate composed a hymn that is still sung today in Egton Bridge at funerals and other occasions. He was visited by many while imprisoned in the condemned cell, and there was for a brief time, hope that he might be spared and simply kept in prison because the authorities were concerned about the effect of wholesale executions for what appeared to be a trivial crime. However, on 11 July 1679, the Privy Council issued an order about 'diverse Popish priests who have been condemned in several counties'. The instruction went on to state that it was 'this day ordered by Their Lordships in Council that the respective judges who go the circuits where the said priests remain do forthwith give direction that they be executed according to the law.'

The day of Father Postgate's execution was set for Thursday, 7 August 1679. Early that morning, he was attended by two ladies Mrs Fairfax, the wife of Charles Fairfax, of York, and Mrs Meynell, of Kilvington, near Thirsk. Both were members of aristocratic families who Father Postgate had served.

Having said his farewells at York Castle, the frail old priest of eighty-two years was then placed on a sledge and hauled along Castlegate, over the Ouse Bridge and up the rough cobbled street of Micklegate. From there he was taken to Knavesmire. Sorrowful Catholics and Protestants lined the route and then, as he await the awful moment, Father Postgate gave his final address.

He told the assembled witnesses that he was dying for the Catholic faith, and not for the Plot. He asked the Sheriff to assure the King that he had never, at any time, wronged His Majesty and prayed God gave the King grace and the light of truth. He forgave all who had in any way done wrong to himself and brought him to his death, and he asked forgiveness for them all. He was then taken away by the executioner. A contemporary account says,

> *You saw him strangled by the hands of the Common* [sic] *Hangman, you saw is head severed from his body, his breast* [sic] *opened and his heart cut out, and the little blood remained in his aged trunk you saw it spilt upon the ground.*

Interestingly, the aftermath of the death of Father Postgate provided as a conclusion, a mystery. His torn and mutilated body was taken away for burial by friends both Catholic and Protestant. It is known that a copper plaque was placed in the coffin that bore these words.

> *Here lyeth that Rd and pious Divine Dr Nicholas Postgate who was educated in the English College at Doway. And after he had labour'd fifty years (to the admirable benefit and conversion of hundrd* [sic] *of souls), was at last advanced to the glorious crown of martyrdom at the city of York on the seventh of August 1679, having been a priest 51 years, aged 81.*[11]

Neither that plaque, nor Father Nicholas Postgate's body has ever been found. As for John Reeves, the unhappy man who apprehended him. He never had the reward that he looked for. But, after having suffered for some time in extreme guilt of mind, his body was found drowned in the stream of Little Beck, recovered from a pool called 'The Devil's Hole' or 'The Devil's Pump', which is still thought to be cursed and where it is said no fish have ever been caught since the informant's death.

Finally, on 5 July 1987, the recently deceased Cardinal Hume, the Cardinal Archbishop of Westminster and late leader of Britain's Roman Catholic community, celebrated Mass at Egton Bridge, in a field adjoining the site of Father Postgate's humble home Kirkdale House. This Mass heralded in Rome the beautification of Nicholas Postgate. In November of that year, eighty-five Roman Catholic martyrs, executed during the sixteenth and seventeenth centuries, were declared Blessed by the Pope in Rome. The beatification of a martyr is considered only one step away from canonization as a saint. Father Nicholas Postgate was one of that number.

Chapter 5

The Pirate Years

nevitably, in earlier times, a coastal plain or coastline was susceptible to pirate raids. Along the coast of Yorkshire this meant attack from Northern Europe and the Scandinavian countries. We have read previously how in the Roman period, the Romans built look-out forts as the first line of defence to give warning and protect the coast and coastal plain against the Norse and Teutonic raiders.

Whitby Abbey was first founded in the year 657. In AD800 it was destroyed and laid waste by Vikings. For nearly two hundred years until the time of the Norman lords it remained in this pitiful state, with a handful of monks eking out an existence in the ruins. Eventually it was refounded by William de Percy, a Norman knight who later became an early abbot of the newly established Benedictine monastery. Yet the monastery, growing as it was both in fame and riches, still had its vicissitudes, for in the time of the second William de Percy we read how:

> *Banditti and plunderers emerged from the woods and their lurking dens, and carried off all the goods of the Monastery, and laid the sacred place itself waste. Pirates also came and pitilessly ravaged and devastated the entire settlement.* [12]

And again, during the rule of the first Abbot Richard, between the years 1148 and 1178 it was written:

> *The King of Norway entered the port of Whitby with many ships, ransacked the goods of the monks, laid waste everything, both within doors and without, and, though he shed no blood, yet he carried off with him whatever he could find; so that they who, by the management of their Abbot, had grown very rich, now became very poor; the rapacious Norwegians having left them nothing.* [13]

Scarborough also suffered from pirate attack (Figure 22). In the year 1377, the first of the reign of King Richard II, a daring Scotch freebooter by the name of Mercer, having been taken by some northern ships, was imprisoned by the Earl of Northumberland, in Scarborough Castle (Figure 23). His son, in revenge for his father's imprisonment, formed a desperate enterprise, and entering the

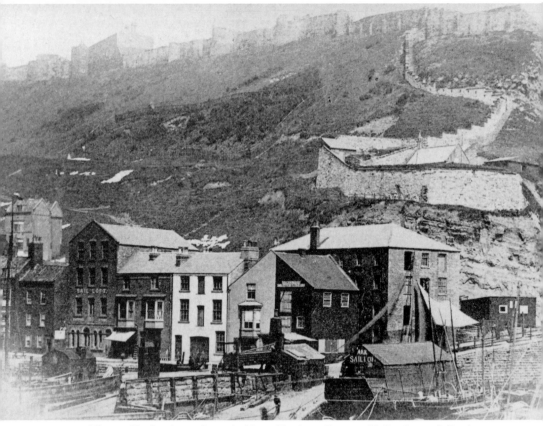

Figure 22. *Scarborough, south side and harbour slipway with Scarborough Castle above.* From an Edwardian postcard.

Figure 23. *Scarborough Castle from the north showing the curtain wall and great keep.*

harbour at Scarborough, with some Scottish, French, and Spanish ships, carried away several merchant vessels which were lying in the port. Encouraged by his success, he for a long period after cruised in the seas round about, and took considerable prizes.

The damage that the merchants sustained by Mercer's depredations, in time occasioned a number of great complaints directed at the government. In response, Alderman John Philpot, an opulent citizen of London, and of a noble and patriotic spirit, resenting so great a national indignity equipped a fleet of armed ships and sailed in pursuit of the Scottish pirate. Within a short time he had the good fortune to encounter Mercer's fleet, and obtained a glorious victory. All the vessels taken from Scarborough were recovered, and fifteen Spanish ships laden with rich merchandise were captured, together with Mercer and the whole of his pirate band.

The gallant Alderman, returning to London in triumph with his prizes, was summarily called by the government to account for his actions. To them the expedition was an usurpation of power. They looked upon it as a dangerous consequence to suffer a private man to engage in such an important affair without permission. But he gave such good reasons, and in so modest a manner, in justification of his enterprise, that he was honourably acquitted, and ever after lived in great esteem and reputation.

Alderman Philpot was elected Lord Mayor of London, in the second year of the reign of King Richard II, and was knighted in the field by the King in 1382, together Sir William Walworth, then Mayor, and four Aldermen, his brethren, for the good services which they performed against Wat Tyler and his accomplices, rebels in Kent. Sir John Philpot also maintained a thousand soldiers at his own charge, for the defence, for the defence of the kingdom against the French, who sorely infested the southern coasts.

During the course of the long French war in the reign of Queen Anne, the inhabitants of Whitby received considerable loss from Dunkirk privateers. Several of their ships were taken, and though most of them were armed with guns in order to put up resistance such actions often resulted in the loss of men. On 22 July 1708, William Boswick was buried in Whitby churchyard, having been shot to death by a French privateer, and there is mention in St Mary's church registers of some others who met their death in the same manner (Figure 24).

Privateers frequently patrolled along the coast to pick up such ships as were badly armed or sailed without convoy. One of these

Figure 24. *The 'Pirates Grave' in the churchyard of St Mary's, Whitby.*

privateers it is said, on a dark winter's night, stood in so close to the cliff, that she came aground at Saltwick, where she remained a considerable time, during which a local man was hired by her crew and dispatched to Whitby. Here he purchased half an anker of ale and returned with the refreshment for the privateers, who sat and drank until their ship was able to float again on the next tide. She got clear off without the alarm being raised or anyone knowing what had happened until it was all over.[14]

The Constable's Accounts show that he paid 2s 6d to four stranded Dutchmen travelling with a pass from Stockton, 'their ship being taken by a privateer being laden with herrings', and at the same time he paid someone the sum of 1s 6d 'for firing ye guns at ye privateer'. Again, on 3 November 1711, he paid 1s 6d for firing guns at a privateer and, on 29 December, another ninepence was paid. Ninepence, to deduce from the Accounts, appears to be the regular price per shot for shooting against privateers.

Canons were placed along the shore and in many seaports to annoy the enemy wherever there was any apprehension of their landing. One of these cannonades was placed on Whitby cliff, on the west side of the harbour, 'which an inhabitant of Whitby, called Thomas Radcliffe, endeavouring to fire at the enemy, in April 1694, it burst and killed him on the spot' (Figure 25).

During the seventeenth century, the lord of the manor of Whiby was a member of the Cholmley family named Sir Hugh. This dynasty had had the lordship for over a hundred years since purchasing the

Figure 25. *The new West Pier Battery, Whitby, in 1796. The two round houses still survive and were used to store gunpowder.*

Figure 26. *Aerial view of the headland Whitby, showing Abbey House and the ruins of Whitby Abbey.*

estate of the monastery after its dissolution by King Henry VIII in 1539. They had built for themselves Abbey House in 1540 on the site of an earlier wooden dwelling. This Abbey House of stone undoubtedly quarried from the adjacent abbey stood above the town overlooking the harbour (Figure 26).

There are several stories of the 'brave Sir Hugh' whose fame was principally acquired 'during those Civil Wars that issued in the wake of the death of King Charles I.' The scene of one of these stories being laid in Whitby harbour, and being moreover, highly characteristic of place, time, and the man, we will give it in his own words.

About June 1683, two Holland men-of-war had chased into Whitby Harbour a small pickroon or vessel belonging to the King of Spain, which had in her only thirty men and two small guns. One of the Hollanders had 400 men, the other 200; and the captains, leaving their ships at anchor in the road, came with their long boats on land, with forty men, every one having his pistols. The Dunkirker, for more security, had put himself above the bridge, and placed his two guns upon his decks, with all his men ready to defend. I, having notice of this, fearing they might do here the like affront as they did at Scarborough, where they landed 100 men, and took a ship belonging to the King of Spain out of the harbour, sent for the Holland captains, and ordered them not to offer any act of hostility; for that the Spaniard was the King's friend, and to have the protection in his ports. After some expostulations, they promised not to meddle with the Dunkirker, if he offered no injury to them; which I gave him strict charge against, and, to trust to the King's protection. These Holland captains leaving me, and going into the town, sent for the Dunkirk captain to dine with them, and soon after took occasion to quarrel with him, at the same time ordered their men to fall on the Dunkirk ship, which they soon surprised, the captain, and most of the crew being absent. I being in my courtyard, and hearing some pistols discharged, and being told the Dunkirkers and Hollanders were at odds, made haste into town, having only a cane in my hand, and one that followed me without any weapon, thinking my presence would pacify all differences. When I came to the riverside, on the sand between the coal-yard and the bridge, I found the Holland captain with a pistol in his hand, calling to his men, then in the Dunkirk ship, to send for a boat. I gave him good words, and held him in treaty until I got near him and then, giving a leap, caught hold of his pistol, which I became master of; yet not without some hazard from the ship, for one there levelled a musket at me; but I espying it, turned the captain between me and him, which prevented his shooting. After I had taken the captain I caused a boat to be manned with men, for retaking the ship; which, as soon as it approached, the Hollanders fled out, and got to their own. In the afternoon I intercepted a letter to the captain, that he should be of good cheer, for at midnight they would have two hundred men and take him away. And in respect they had by force taken a Dunkirk ship not long before out of Scarborough Harbour. I conjectured they might be bold here; and therefore gave notice to Sir John Hotham, of Fyling, then High Sheriff of the county, who came to me, and summoned all the adjacent train-bands. We had I think two hundred men on guard that night; but then, so inexpert, that not one among them except a few seamen knew at all how to handle their arms, or discharge a musket; and it had been happy for this nation that they had continued till now in that ignorance. These ships continued hovering before the harbour for two or three days, till I sent the captain to York; who was after sent to London, by order from the Privy Council, who approved of me laying hold of him, and gave me thanks for it. I think he remained prisoner nearly two years before the Prince Palatine came over and obtained his release.

Chapter 6

A Civil War Traitor –
Captain Browne Bushell (c.1609-51)

I n 1633, Captain Browne Bushell married a daughter of Sir Thomas Fairfax, Oliver Cromwell's Chief of Staff, who had alum works at Dunsley. He brought his bride to Bagdale Hall at Whitby, a house built in the reign of King Henry VIII, and which at that time was said to stand 'near unto Whitby' (Figure 27). At the date of his marriage in 1633, Bushell was aged twenty-four years his bride was sixteen.

Centuries later, in 1916, the then owner of Bagdale Hall, Percy Shaw Jeffery, the widely-travelled, philanthropic, retired headmaster of Colchester Grammar School, Freeman of the City of London, and author of *Whitby Lore and Legend*, discovered two portraits painted in oils on board in the roof loft of his new home. When they were found, both paintings were in a perilous condition, literally in pieces and unrecognisable. They were sent to London for expert treatment, the component pieces were screwed together again and cleaned, and after restoration, each picture was found to be dated 1633, and have the age of each of the persons on their respective portraits.

Figure 27. *Bagdale Hall in 1920, before the road was redeveloped.*

Figure 28. *The bride of Captain Browne Bushell in 1633, oil on wood panel.*

Figure 29. *A portrait of Captain Browne Bushell in 1633, oil on wood panel.*

Each of the sitters wears a betrothal ring hanging by a chain round the neck. The handsome man is in court dress and wears a sword, while the bride carries a prayer book in the right hand, and wears a ruff and an elaborately pleated mob-cap (Figure 28).

The experts who restored the pictures pronounced them to be the work of some itinerant Dutch painter name unknown, and they were returned to their new owners with the following significant comment:

> *These two portraits show very fine execution, and whatever price you gave for your house, the value of the portraits should more than recoup you for your outlay.*

The man is undoubtedly Captain Browne Bushell, who subsequently became Whitby's most feared and infamous sea pirate (Figure 29). The other, for many years, was innocently believed to be his bride, Elizabeth Fairfax. That she was indeed his wife is probable; that she was Elizabeth is most unlikely. Her identity remains a mystery, but what is now certain is that she cannot be the daughter of Sir Thomas Fairfax if the age of the woman is correct. If this is so, the young bride would have been born in 1616/17, and therefore could not have been the daughter of either Sir Thomas, Parliament's famous general, who was born in 1612, or of Thomas Fairfax, of Dunsley, the Royalist, whose daughter was born in 1605.

If Browne Bushell was in the Netherlands between 1632 and 1642, which is likely, then the portraits may well have been painted in that country. Experts agree that they were painted in the Dutch style. The absence from Yorkshire of his marriage licence suggests that this event took place elsewhere. Did Captain Bushell have another wife of Dutch nationality before returning to England? We may never know.

Captain Browne Bushell is always supposed to have been baptised in Whitby Parish Church sometime in May 1609 and said to have possibly been born at Ruswarp Old Hall. His father was Nicholas Bushell, gentleman, wealthy merchant and owner of Bagdale Hall and Ruswarp Old Hall (Figure 30). Browne Bushell in the Whitby parish Registers is described as 'being of Whitby'. His Christian name came from his maternal grandmother, whose maiden name was Browne. His mother was Dorothy Cholmley, daughter of Sir Henry Cholmley, head of the most powerful family in the district.

Figure 30. *Ruswarp Old Hall, front elevation.*

His cousin was Sir Hugh Cholmley.

On the death of his father, Nicholas, Browne Bushell took his share from the sale of Bagdale Hall and became a soldier of fortune firstly offering his services to the King of Spain. He was an 'officer adventurer' in the continental Thirty Years' War (1618-48), like many English gentlemen of the time. His profession then, of mercenary, was considered an honourable one, fit for a gentleman of spirit, but without financial means. War at that period was considered a 'finishing school' for men, an alternative to university or the legal profession and time at one of the London Inn's of Court.

Browne Bushell was abroad for ten years, and but for the outbreak of Civil War in England he might never have returned home. The beginning of the 'distractions' as they were known by his profession, brought him back from Dunkirk in 1642. During this period he had a chequered military career.

He firstly joined the side of Parliament against King Charles I not out of any political or religious conviction, but probably because it was the first side to offer him a commission. Men with his military experience were now highly valued in a country used to peace. He was given command of 36-gun warship, Martin, and sent to attack the Royalist forces who were holding Portsmouth.

Parliament's faith in Captain Bushell was not misplaced. In a succession of bold and enterprising assaults he so undermined the morale of the King's men that they mutinied against their colonel and forced him to surrender the town and valuable harbour. One of Bushell's night-time exploits was to swim the moat of Southsea Castle, climb its thirty-foot high wall and, with only one companion, persuade its startled garrison to surrender without resistance.

Captain Browne Bushell next turned up at Scarborough and served under his cousin Sir Hugh Cholmley who held the garrison for Parliament in 1643. During his period at Scarborough his military experience was put to strengthening the defences. Today, Bushell's Battery, the name given to an outworks at Scarborough Castle near the entrance to the castle gate that he built, and on which he stood artillery that exchanged fire with the Royalists artillery formed up in the church and churchyard of nearby St Mary's, reminds us of his presence there.

It was in March of 1643, however, that Cholmley made a decision to change sides and become a Royalist and to hand over the castle at Scarborough to Queen Henrietta, wife of Charles I, who was then at York helping her beleagued husband. In turn, after some hesitation, Captain Browne Bushell changed sides with him, although he still held Scarborough Castle for Parliament. While travelling to York to make arrangements about the surrender of Scarborough Castle, Cholmley sent his kinsman Bushell to Hull to fetch some valuables that he had in store there. Bushell sailed to Hull in a small pinnance mounted with seven small guns for protection. Unfortunately, at Hull he was taken by the Governor Sir John Hotham, who, ironically, was also a cousin and who was not entirely convinced of his new-found loyalty to the Royalist cause. He held Bushell prisoner for two days, after which he was released on a promise to deliver Scarborough Castle to the cavaliers.

Interestingly, it was his cousin Sir Hugh Cholmley who was given the task of taking the castle from Bushell. Sir Hugh Cholmley, now a Royalist, stayed the night 'at a little inn called the Falsgrave' and invited Bushell to meet with him next morning.

The two Whitby men met outside the Newborough Bar (Figure 31). Bushell then opened the town gates and gave Sir Hugh the keys to the castle. Eight years later when King Charles I was dead and Cromwell was in power, this was seen as an act of treason by the Parliamentarians and he was to die on Tower Hill for betraying Scarborough to the enemy 'without making any resistance or discharging any shot'.

From this point on, Captain Browne Bushell became an increasingly painful thorn in the side of Cromwell's forces. He plundered Lord Mulgrave's estate; he seized ships in Whitby

Figure 31. *The successor to the original Newborough Bar c.1885, designed by the architect Barry in the mid-nineteenth century.*

harbour, putting one of their master's in irons; and he chased the Roundheads all the way back from Beverley to Hull.

It is then said, that on hearing that his father-in-law, Sir Thomas Fairfax had been sent to arrest him, he changed back to the side of Parliament. On being taken by Fairfax, who sent him under escort to London, he was able to satisfy his accusers that he was a staunch supporter of the Parliamentarian cause. This was on 19 April 1645 when he was thirty-six years of age and in the closing years of the reign of King Charles I.

He was next given captaincy of a Parliamentarian ship under the Fleet command of Admiral Sir William Batten. When, in early 1648, the Fleet lay in the Downs, Bushell and several other ship captains decided that the tide was turning against Cromwell and so delivered their ships to the Prince of Wales and once again, Bushell took up the King's cause.

When the Parliamentarian troops began to win control of the land, the Captain took to the sea in a 12-gun, 750-ton ship called the *Cavendish*, and took to gun running and finally, piracy. It is said of all the 'sea-rovers' that preyed on Cromwell's North Sea ships, none was more notorious than 'the Bushell'. Collier boats dare not put to sea from Newcastle for fear of him. London ran short of winter coal because of his attacks. Hardly a week passed at one period without some newspaper complaining of Bushell's impudence. Parliament that had once praised his courage now cried out for his capture and offered a reward of twenty pounds for his apprehension.

Even when Scarborough town and harbour fell to the Roundheads in 1645, Captain Browne Bushell was not taken. The *Exchange Intelligencer* reported angrily that 'the perfidious apostate' was 'now robbing up and down our coasts' out of Dunkirk.

When the Civil War finally finished with Parliament winning in 1646, Captain Browne Bushell did not ask for pardon. To him there seemed little point. Homeless and without estate, unlike his cousin, Sir Hugh Cholmley who recanted and once again became a Parliamentarian in order to save his home and lands at Whitby, he was by this time a professional buccaneer, too rootless and restless to become a law-abiding citizen ever again. When the French chased him and his fellow captains out of Boulogne in the following year, he changed his base of operations to Jersey.

Eventually Captain Browne Bushell met his match in 1648. Raiding off Tynemouth, he was caught by Captain John Lawson, of Scarborough who later attained the rank of Admiral and was knighted. The welcome news of Bushell's capture was reported to the

Figure 32. *The House of Commons in the seventeenth century, from an engraving by John Glover.*

House of Commons by General Cromwell (Figure 32). The 'old sea pirate' as the *Parliament's Post* had once described him, had finally been netted.

He was imprisoned in Windsor Castle, and the governor was instructed 'to keep him very strict and safe, as he will answer the same at his peril'. On 20 December 1649, however, the Council of Cromwell's Parliament considered a complaint by Bushell alleging improper treatment. It was ordered that the governor 'provide for him as necessary for one of his quality'. In the following year, on 26 June, he was allowed five shillings a week to make his imprisonment more bearable.

Figure 33. *The eighteenth century execution block erected on Tower Hill.*

In total it took three years to gather evidence against the Captain and only one day to prove his guilt by trial in Westminster Hall. A note in the records of the House of Commons reads:

The question being propounded that Captain Browne Bushell be excepted [arraigned] and tried for his life, the House was divided: Yeas 26, Noes 17.

He was condemned to die on the anniversary of his surrender of Scarborough Castle.

An eyewitness left a vivid description of Bushell's last minutes on Tower Hill, where he was executed on Saturday, 29 March 1651 (Figure 33). Promptly, at five o'clock in the afternoon, he emerged from the Tower of London wearing a red cloak. He took off his hat respectfully and addressed the enormous crowd of spectators that had gathered to witness his final moments.

Still unrepentant, he told the assembly that his only regret was to have been on the wrong side at the start of the war. He declared himself to be a true son of the Church of England.

THE
SPEECH
AND
Confeffion of Capt. Brown-Bufhel, at the place of Execution on *Saturday* laft, und r the Scaffold on Tower-Hill : With the manner of his deportment, and his coming from the Tower in a Scarlet Cloak ; as alfo his Prayer, and Defires to the People. Together with the manner of his Tryall ; and the Articles and Charge exbibited againft him.

Written by G. H. an Eye-Witneffe.

Imprinted at *London* by R. W. 1 6 5 1.

Turning to the executioner, he asked him if it was the same axe and block which had been used to execute the King, Charles I. When he was told, yes, Bushell seemed pleased. He produced twenty shillings and gave these to the axe-man saying that he wished it had been more. He then removed his cloak and doublet, donned a white cap which he pulled from his pocket, and knelt at the block (Figure 34). Seconds later Captain Browne Bushell became a Royalist martyr.

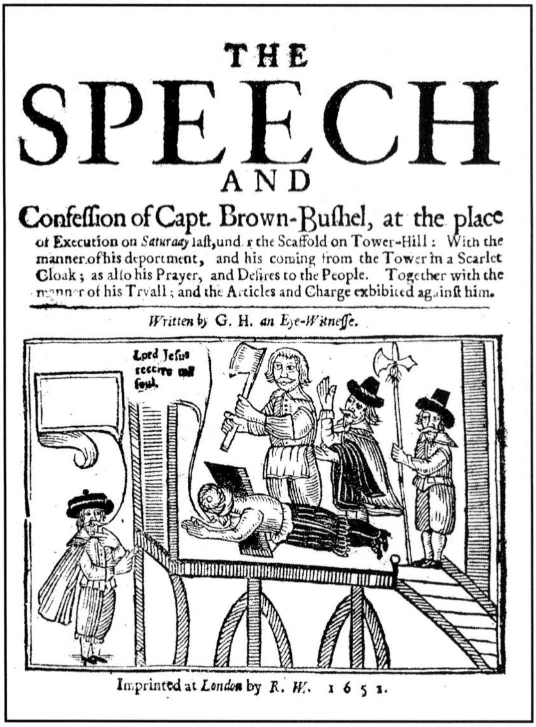

Figure 34. *The illustrated cover, dated 1651, showing the execution of Captain Browne Bushell on Tower Hill.*

Chapter 7

'Til Death us do Part! –

Reverend Henock Sinclair (d.1708)

Themes following tale tells of the murder of the Reverend Henock Sinclair, Vicar of Owthorne, who was killed by his servant.

At the time of the incident, the vicar's household consisted of himself, his two nieces Mary and Catherine Sinclair, and a male servant, Adam Alvin. Together they lived in the vicarage at Owthorne, now one of the lost villages of the East Coast that stood near to Withernsea before the waves took it away.

Local tradition has it that Adam, when a mere babe, was washed up on the beach with his mother from the wreck of a ship. The mother clung tenaciously to her infant and rendered it all the protection she could. She did not recover the ordeal, however, but her child seemed little the worse. Then arose the question of what was to be done with the baby, and as none of the vicar's poor parishioners appeared able to take in another child, and there were no workhouses or charitable institutions at that time, the vicar himself took it to his own house. As no one claimed the child he stayed on at the vicarage, and the vicar taught him such elements of

As the lad grew older he was occupied in the vicarage garden or in any odd work about the house, or in assisting the vicar's two nieces who had been living with the Reverend Sinclair for some years. In short he was put to work as a general manservant. The youth was of a somewhat morose and sulky disposition, but somehow, by his extra attention to Mary, the elder of the two nieces, he gained her affections. This in the course of time could not be hid from the vicar, who raised strong objections to what he conceived to be a very ill assorted match. The young folks, however, were bent on having their own way, and as the vicar's objections continued to be pressed, Alvin seems to have conceived the idea of getting rid of the vicar in order to marry Mary. His outbursts of temper were frequent, and by degrees both the nieces became aware of the sinister feelings which Adam Alvin harboured against their uncle.

On 4 May 1708 the vicar attended a parish vestry meeting, at which was laid a 'Tax for ye Overseer's of [the] Poore by ye inhabitants of Owthorne'. This tax assessment was set at 3d in the pound, and the list of parishioners and the amount of rate due from each, was noted in the Churchwarden's Account Book in the Reverend Sinclair's usual very neat handwriting.

About five weeks after this vestry meeting, the vicar was found murdered in the vicarage house, slain by Adam Alvin. Whether the act was fully premeditated or was done by an altercation with the vicar is unknown. Whatever, the events thereafter were definitely premeditated, when the body was buried in the vicarage garden, and the vicar's horse, saddled and bridled as for a journey, was taken out of the stable and left some miles from the village. A report was then circulated that the vicar had set out on a journey the previous day, and had disappeared, probably over the cliff (the old vicarage at that time being close to the sea), as his hat and wig were found on the beach (thrown there by Alvin) (Figure 35). This report, however, did not appear to have had credibility in the village, and as Adam Alvin was by no means a favourite with the villagers, ugly rumours began to spread associating his name with a crime of murder. Alvin, however, had enjoined silence on the part of the two women in the household, no doubt on the pretext of love, one for the love of her man, the other, for the love of her sister, and as no one else knew of his actions, nothing could be proven against him.

His next step was to marry Mary Sinclair, and, as it might not have been safe to have had the ceremony in their own parish, it was arranged it should take place at Halsham, six miles distant. In order that the approaching wedding might be kept as secret as possible, a licence was obtained, which, of course, did away with the necessity for publication of the banns, and the ceremony took place at Halsham on 29 August 1708, only two or three months after the demise of the uncle.

After some time, Adam Alvin and his wife left the neighbourhood to reside in London.

Four years after the murder, Catherine Sinclair had a serious illness, and to ease her conscience, she either made a full confession of the events, or gave such indications as led to the discovery of the body in the vicarage grounds. Alvin and his wife were then arrested in London and brought to York for trial. Adam Alvin was convicted of the murder of the Reverend Henock Sinclair, his wife was acquitted. During the trial Alvin protested his innocence to the end. However, faced with death on the morning of his execution, he confessed the crime.

At the trial, it was never clearly established what exactly was the motive for the vicar's murder. Most thought it was because of the

Figure 35. *Owthorne church in 1800 from Thompson's* Ocellum Promontorium, *showing the close proximity to the cliff edge, and in the distance (right) the old vicarage.*

uncle's objections to their union. There is, however, an additional piece of documentary evidence that was never brought to light at the time. In the Owthorne Overseers' Book, the rate which had already been referred to as laid down and listed on 4 May 1708, was headed by the name of the vicar in respect of a property worth annually £12. In the year following the murder, Mr Sinclair's name drops out, and the name of Adam Alvin, in right of his wife, came into some property on the death of the vicar; but whether the crime originated in Alvin's resentment at the vicar's objections to the marriage, or in a desire to gain possession of this property, will probably never be known.

Chapter 8

Yo! Ho! Ho! And a Bottle of Rum – Smugglers' Tales

muggling activities, prevalent along the coast hereabouts for many years, inevitably gave rise to violent action. In June 1776, men of the 1st Royal British Dragoons, stationed at York, and on detachment to assist the Riding Officers, were involved when the Customs Officer of Whitby made a seizure of contraband which after a struggle with the smugglers, was safely lodged in the Excise Warehouse at Whitby next morning (Figure 36). On this occasion, as reported in a newspaper dated 16 June 1776, events turned extremely nasty and murder ensued. What occurred was briefly as follows:

> *A smuggling cutter boat, laden with geneva, went on shore at Runswick. The Officer of the Customs there, with four Privates of the 1st Regiment of Dragoons, took possession of the boat. The men belonging to her, seeing what had happened, went to the Customs House and negotiated with the Customs Officer and soldiers that they should have all the liquor provided they would relinquish the boat, and prevailed on the Dragoons to discharge their pistols. No sooner had this been done than the smugglers rose up and attacked the soldiers so cruelly that one of them died the next morning from wounds received. He had been nineteen years in the regiment and had fought through four campaigns in Germany. The Customs Officer saved himself by fleeing. A Coroner's Jury returned a verdict of 'wilful murder' against the smugglers.*

The smugglers formed part of the forty-strong crew of the *Kent* captained by the notorious swashbuckling George 'Stoney' Fagg. A reward of one hundred pounds was offered for their capture. Eventually Stoney Fagg and the *Kent*, a good sized vessel of 200 tons with a 77 foot high main mast and main boom of 57 feet, and heavily armed with sixteen four-pounder carriage-mounted cannon, twenty swivel-guns, and blunderbusses, was captured off Filey in July of the following year (Figure 37).

The manner in which the *Kent* met its end and 'Stoney' Fagg was captured involved a considerable battle. It took two Revenue Sloops, the *Prince of Wales* and the *Royal George* attached to the Scottish

Figure 36. *Whitby harbour, looking toward Grape Lane and Sandgate (left) as it would have been in 1776. The Customs House and warehouse at this date was in Sandgate.*

Figure 37. *The eighteenth century schooner,* Kent, *commanded by captain George 'Stoney' Fagg.*

Excise Board, and two naval frigates to get her. One of these, HMS *Pelican* had chased the *Kent* out of Bridlington Bay the day before and lost her during the night. The two excise boats came upon her next day off Filey. Fagg shouted 'Fire and be damned to you!' The battle had lasted an hour when the *Pelican* came on the scene, but the *Kent* still managed to evade capture until the other Royal Navy ship HMS *Arethusa* entered the affray. Between them all, eventually the *Kent* was boarded and George 'Stoney' Fagg was taken along with 'the murderers of the Dragoons at Whitby the previous year'.

At Staithes in 1777, there was an affray between the smugglers and troops, during which a Trooper, Casseldine, died from injuries received (Figure 38). The Attorney for the Customs in Whitby and Mr Spink, Customs Officer for Whitby, had difficulty in finding any witnesses except the three other Dragoons involved, although several local people had seen the event from a distance and these were called

Figure 38. *Staithes, North Yorkshire, in 1898.*

unwillingly to give evidence. There was no doubt that the soldier had been struck a blow on the head with a stick when lying on the ground by Richard Curtis, of Staithes. The surgeon, Mr Leonard, told the Attorney that he saw the deceased two days after death, and that he found a great many bruises all over the body and a great quantity of blood congealed below his ribs on the left side, as if some blood vessels had been broken by the violence of the blow, and that a bruise in the head proved to be a complete fracture over his left eye. This latter injury would have caused death in four or five days, but the other injuries could have hastened the soldiers demise. He could not say what kind of weapon was used, but Spink, apparently present at the affray, stated that Richard Curtis had a bludgeon and that the other smugglers were armed similarly and with pistols. The surgeon made it clear that there was no wounds inflicted by any other weapon, therefore it was probable that the bruises were made by bludgeons or the butt end of pistols.

The accused came up for trial at York in July 1778. Unfortunately, the murder charged failed. Afterwards Mr J Burgh, the Collector, wrote to Mr George Lichfield, Solicitor of the Customs, reporting that all the evidence had been given satisfactorily

> except Mr Leonard, the Surgeon, who deviated extremely upon the trial from what he had advanced to the Attorney, in consequence whereof Curtis was found not guilty of murder, but on account of the smuggling was suffered by the Judge to enter His Majesty's sea service.

In 1784 there was a serious riot in Whitby when feelings ran high against the Press Gang and their method of taking recruits. The headquarters of the Press Gang at that time was in Haggersgate, in an inn kept by Joseph Cooper (Figure 39). The inn was an old timber-framed building and early in that year a mob of local sailors and others congregated in the street and proceeded to pull the place down. Inside were Press Gang men of the Royal Navy under the command of a Lieutenant Atkinson. The ensuing battle was a savage affair in which bricks, stones, capstan bars and clubs were freely employed and, once the door had been beaten down, the whole interior was gutted. An attempt the following night to burn down what was left was stopped by the arrival of the Military.

After the dust had settled, interestingly, only one man was carried off to York Castle to pay the price for the rioting, seventy-year old William Atkinson, who was charged with inciting a riot and aiding an abetting. He was publicly hung at York on Saturday, 12 April 1790

Figure 39. *Haggersgate, Whitby in the nineteenth century. The* Elephant & Castle *public house still survives, renamed* The Star.

Figure 40. *A public execution behind York Castle, from Drake's* History of York.

protesting to the last that he had no part in the events (Figure 40).

In a previous century Thomas Langdale, aged twenty-seven, a native of Scarborough, was executed at York, with nine others, on 4 February, 1634, for rioting about corn at Hull, and demolishing the dwelling house of Edward Cooper, and taking therefrom a quantity of clothing.[15]

Figure 41. *An eighteenth century public notice announcing the arrest of various 'coiners'.*

Sept 16, 1769

C O I N E R S

COMMITTED TO

YORK CASTLE,

ON SUSPICION

Of Chipping, Filing, Edging, and Diminishing the Gold Coin of this Kingdom.

ON Wednesday evening, the 6th instant, was committed to York Castle, Jonn Pickles, of Wadfworth Banks, near Halifax, on fufpicion of diminishing three guineas, and one twenty feven shilling piece of Portugal gold : After he was feized there were found in his pockets, a pair of fciffars, and an instrument for milling the edges of gold pieces. At the time the above delinquent was apprehended, he was manufacturing white pieces, and feemed to leave his Looms very reluctantly : He is an elderly man, near fixty, has a wife and large family, and it is fuppofed he is an old offender.

Alfo on Friday laft was committed to York Caftle, John Sutclyffe, of Erringden, in the Weft Riding, charged with chipping, filing, edging, and diminishing feveral guineas, and a half a guinea.

Alfo on Saturday laft, in the evening, ——— Oldfield, of Midgley, was committed to York Caftle, for clipping, coining, &c. &c.

' Laft night in the evening, the wife of John Pickles, commonly called Jack of Matts, alias Jack of Packet Well, was conducted thro' this town, (Halifax) on her way to York Caftle, on horfeback, with her hands ty'd, and coining tools in a bag by her fide. As fhe paff'd thru' the bottom of the town, the man who led the horfe danced, and the mob hooted her over the bridge. This woman has

been the moft noted vender and procurer in thefe parts.

, At the time fhe was taken, her hufband made his efcape ; fhe likewife declared, fhou'd her hufband be taken and fuffer the law, that wou'd, (thro' her information,) hang forty coiners.

This day feveral perfons of this town and parts adjacent, have abfconded, as is fuppofed for fear of being apprehended.

It is alfo confidently afferted that there have been above ONE HUNDRED perfons informed of, and that there are now Warrants out againft the moft confiderable of them.

We have now the pleafing fatisfaction of feeing the Bands of thefe formidable fet of villains broken : Terror and difmay have taken holden of them, and they no longer care face the injured public.

Behold Great Turvin, fee the Time draw near, When every Golden Sun fhall Quake with Fear, See Tyburn gorged with protr.fted Fond, And honour'd with the Wright of * Royal Blood.

* Alluding to fome of the COINERS being called KINGS.

A WALL POSTER ANNOUNCING THE ARREST OF COINERS.

In the same period of history, Arthur Mangey, aged sixty-eight years, a goldsmith, of Leeds, was executed at York on 30 March 1696, for counterfeiting the current coin of the realm (Figure 41). He was drawn to his place of execution on a hurdle in the presence of a large concourse of spectators. After the execution, his body was given to friends to be interred at Leeds. Mangey was connected in coining transactions with John Brown, a whitesmith, at Scarborough, and Robert Child, blockmaker, of Scarborough, also executed. A notorious coiner, named Woodhouse, of York, also belonged to the gang.[16]

'Clipping' coins was a serious crime for many years, and involved shaving off a small piece of the edge of a gold coin, the shavings of which, when having amount to a considerable portion, where then sold. It was because of this practise, that the milled edge was introduced on coins so that it would be easily noticed whether a gold coin had been 'clipped' or shaved.

Chapter 9

The Legend of Saltersgate

ention has been made of the Lilla Cross. For years it formed part of a series of such crosses that guided travellers over the North Yorkshire moors from Robin Hood's Bay to the many remote scattered moorland communities such Saltersgate. In medieval times, there were numerous tracks across the moors used by merchants and pack-horse traders carrying goods, and many of these tracks used the Lilla Cross as a waymarker. It was not until the eighteenth century that some of these ancient tracks began to take on a new permanence and others were laid down. The present route from Whitby to Pickering for instance, did not exist until 1759, when it was created as an extension of the first road to be built in the Whitby district.[17] This very first route out of that seaport ran from Whitby to Saltersgate, an indication of the importance of that village at one time.

In the seventeenth and eighteenth centuries, there was a constant procession of fishermen with strings of horses and carts bearing loads of herrings trekking from the coast inland. From Robin Hood's Bay they made use of the old Fish Road sometimes known as the Salt Road. This route was based on an ancient medieval track that led from the coast via John Cross Rigg, Blea Hill Beck and over the Green Swang to Lilla Howe. From there the route crossed Lilla Rigg beside the cross and then ran via Worm Sike Rigg and Loose Howe until it met a rough track that ran across the bleak moors from Whitby. Some remains of that ancient Fish Road now form footpaths and still survive.

But why should these fishermen have been travelling so far from the sea with their catches? The reason was salt. Fisherman needed salt to preserve the fish, especially when it had to be transported great distances from Whitby and Robin Hood's Bay to markets. So a brisk trade in the smuggling of salt was established. Until January 1825, salt was heavily taxed. An excise duty of ten shillings a bushel had been imposed in 1798, rising to fifteen shillings by 1805. It was reduced to two shillings in 1823 then abolished soon afterwards. A bushel measured eight gallons, this form of measurement being used for salt, and fifteen shillings would be around a month's wages for a farm labourer. This illustrates the excessive nature of the tax. At its

Figure 42. Saltersgate Inn, *near Whitby, as it is today, and which was formerly named the* Wagon & Horses.

height between 1798 and 1805, there was a massive amount of salt-smuggling carried on in and around the North Yorkshire moors, with Customs and Excise Officers constantly alert for smugglers, and for those who traded illegally in salt or liquor.

The focal point for salt smuggling inland from Whitby and Robin Hoods Bay was a remote moorland inn called the *Wagon and Horses*. Erected in 1648, it stood in the centre of a huge expanse of wilderness at the edge of Lockton High Moor, but in the shelter of a steep hill below the rim of the Hole of Horcum. Several ancient tracks met here and a number of cottages and farms surrounded the inn, but it was, and still is, noted for its solitude and it was the only accessible ascent from the lower moors up to the high plateau of Lockton Moor above. Today, that same inn stands beside the A169 Pickering - Whitby moor road and is known as the *Saltersgate Inn* (Figure 42).

It was here that a murder took place around the year 1800, though the exact date is uncertain. The salt tax was at its highest rate and many made use of the isolation of the inn to carry on their trade of illegally salting fish. Large amounts of a salt were brought here by traders and secreted in the cellars. The beams contained rows of fish hooks while the inn's many cupboards built into the wall around the fireplaces were used to store salt so that its was always dry and ready for use.

At the beginning of the nineteenth century a group of fishermen from Robin Hood's Bay began a journey across the deserted moor with a load of fish to be salted at the *Wagon and Horses*. By this date, there was an increase in the traffic passing Saltersgate because of the new road which had been built in 1759, and because in general, the effect of the *Turnpike Acts* of that period, was to provide better roads that allowed for coaches and faster travelling by horse. But the fishermen travelled at night so that the darkness would shelter their movements. It was the custom at the *Wagon and Horses* to put a light in a small window on the south-facing wall to warn of the presence of Customs and Excise Officers. The absence of a light meant that it was safe to approach. As the group of Bay fishermen approached the lonely inn, they saw no light in the tiny window and so continued in their expedition.

Unfortunately, a single Excise Officer whose name is now unknown, was lying in wait and no one knew of his presence. No light was placed in the window to warn off the small party of fishermen. They arrived and the concealed Excise Officer waited until he could obtain firm evidence of their illicit purpose, finally creeping down into the cellar as the fish-salting was in progress. After months of investigation, he had caught the fishermen and innkeeper in the act and had succeeded in obtaining all the evidence he required. The Excise Officer, however, was destined never to leave that inn, dead or alive.

A tremendous fight ensued, during which the Officer was killed; whether this was done deliberately or by accident has never been determined. Notwithstanding, for the fishermen, they knew that the death of a lone Excise Officer going about his lawful duty brought about by a party undertaking illegal business would be regarded as murder if the authorities ever heard about it. Everyone knew the penalty - death by hanging. After some thought it was decided to cover up their crime. After all, travellers did get lost upon those moors; many lone horseman and solitary footman died and were never seen again, their bodies left to rot among the deep heather, so who could prove that the Excise Officer had ever reached the inn?

Confident that their crime would go undetected the fisherman and the innkeeper agreed upon a conspiracy of silence and decided to

Figure 43. *The fireplace in the* Wagon & Horses, *Saltersgate - 'The fire that never goes out' - the message on the reverse says, 'charabanc trip to here, had some of there cakes straight from oven'.*

bury the corpse beneath the hearth of the fire. And so it was done; their deed would never be known. Very soon afterwards in 1800, a new fireplace and fireside range was built into the bar of the inn by Dobsons, of Pickering, and this is the one that can be seen today (Figure 43).

As for the Excise Officer, he is still said to be incarcerated beneath the fireplace. And from the day he was put under its great stone hearth a turf fire has burned continually in the grate and a legend has arisen that if it does go out, the ghost of the Excise Officer will return to haunt the inn. Today the *Wagon and Horses* under its present name of the *Saltersgate Inn* continues to prove accommodation and refreshment for travellers, many of whom sit and gaze into the historic old fireplace whose flame has burned for nearly two hundred years. But does the body of the murdered Excise Officer lie beneath it and if so, who killed him? No one was ever brought to justice despite the search and investigation that followed after rumours began to circulate about his disappearance, perhaps we will never know.

Chapter 10

The Hand of Glory

The 'Hand of Glory' is a gruesome relic of nineteenth century criminal history. It was used as a charm in many parts of Europe by burglars, and also by sorcerers. It consisted of the hand of a hanged felon, cut from the body as it hung on the gibbet, pickled with various salts, and dried in strong sunlight or in an oven until it was quite hard. It was then employed as a candleholder for a candle made of a hanged man's fat, virgin wax, and Lapland sesame (Figure 44).[18]

Thus prepared, it had the power of stupefying those to whom it was displayed, and rendered persons motionless, 'in such a way that they can no more stir than if they were dead.'[19] Thieves believed that if the 'Hand of Glory' was brought into a house at night, and the candle lit, none of the sleeping inmates would awaken while it burnt.

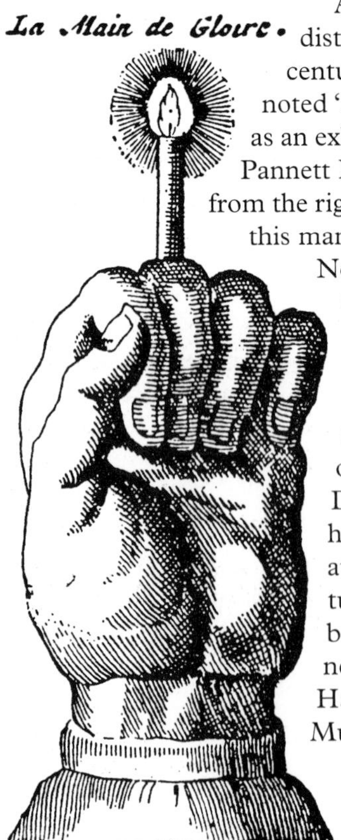

La Main de Gloire.

Around Whitby and the surrounding district such superstitions predominated for centuries, and particularly at Danby was a noted 'Hand of Glory' which finally came to rest as an exhibit in the museum at Whitby situated in Pannett Park. It is a genuine human hand severed from the right arm of a hanged criminal, though who this man was is not known.

Nor is it known how the Danby 'Hand of Glory' survived after 1820 when it was last thought to have been used, but by chance it came into the possession of an antiquarian in the village. He kept it for many years and as he approached the end of his life, he considered burying it in Danby churchyard (Figure 45). Instead, he passed it to the Eskdale historian and author Joseph Ford (1870-1944) who in turn passed it to another friend, having been given an assurance that it would never be lost to posterity. Today, the Danby Hand of Glory is safe within Whitby Museum, taken there from the cottage of a

Figure 44. *An illustration of the 'Hand of Glory' from an ancient French textbook on magic. The first mention of this grisly relic was in the fifteenth century.*

Figure 45. *The church of St Hilda, Danby and churchyard.* Whitby Gazette

Figure 46. *A view of Danby with Danby water-powered corn mill in the foreground (left).*

Dr Chalmers who lived at Castleton near to Danby.

The village of Danby lies in the North York Moors National Park (Figure 46). The village and its surrounding countryside were immortalized by Canon J C Atkinson (1814-1900), a vicar of Danby, in a classic Yorkshire book entitled *Forty Years in a Moorland Parish*. Danby is also home of the Moors Centre run by the National Park, and here a wealth of information and exhibits can be found on the area and the work of the National Park Committee. The Moors Centre, formerly known as Danby Lodge, was once a royal hunting lodge converted from a sixteenth century farmhouse.

In addition to the beautiful countryside, Danby also played a small part in the history of the nation, for it is here that the partial ruins of Danby Castle stand, perched on the side of Danby Rigg. This was the seat of the Latimer family, and it was here that the sixth and last wife of King Henry VIII, Catherine Parr lived out her days. Open to the public as well as being a working farm, in one of its rooms sit the ancient Danby Court Leet that has jurisdiction over the rights of way and common land in the parish. It is one of only thirty-eight Court Leet which survive in England and one of four within the North Yorks moors. Below, in the shadow of Danby Castle, runs the river Esk, and spanning it at this point is an ancient narrow attractive pack-horse bridge named Duck Bridge erected around the year 1386 (Figure 47).

Figure 47. *Duck Bridge, Danby, and the coat of arms of the Neville family (inset) which can be seen carved into the stonework of the parapet.*

Figure 48. *A hanged man on the gallows from which the 'Hand of Glory' would be severed.*

Until the middle years of the nineteenth century, there were many 'Hands of Glory', most used by burglars as they committed their crimes. Most superstitious criminals would obtain their own hand, and the only source was the body of a felon hanging upon the gibbet (Figure 48). It was also believed that a severed hand could cure many diseases. Throughout medieval times in this country and abroad, a belief developed that the hand of a hanged man, or that of any person who had committed suicide, possessed strong magical or curative powers. For this reason, gibbets and gallows were often raided after hanging, either to remove the dead hand or to touch oneself with it. The strength of these beliefs often meant that the hand had to be severed in secret. Some took ladders, others relied on friends to assist them reach the swinging hand which they drew across the effected part, perhaps three, seven or nine times, each being a magic number.

In the main, however, the 'Hand of Glory' was chiefly employed by burglars going about their nefarious deeds, although in the year 1588, there is an account of a trial where two alleged witches used a 'Hand of Glory' while poisoning their victims in the belief it would prevent their capture.

The use of such a charm or talisman by a criminal was of great importance. The crime of burglary was classified as a felony and carried the death penalty. This penalty continued until 1837 when the death penalty was limited to cases where violence had been committed against a person during burglary, and in 1861 the penalty was reduced to penal servitude for life. Until 1967, the crime of burglary was defined as breaking into dwelling-houses during the hours of darkness.[20]

To undertake burglary before the year 1837, therefore, meant risking life, and so of course, any means of reducing that risk was employed. The 'Hand of Glory' was one of these means. It is interesting to note that the use of the 'Hand of Glory' declined around the period of criminal reforms and when the death penalty ceased to be the punishment for convicted burglars. The last recorded use of a 'Hand of Glory' was in 1831.[21]

An account of this robbery appeared in *The Observer* of 16 January 1831. It took place at Loughcrew, county Meath, in Ireland at the house of a Mr Napier.

> *The burglars entered the house armed with a dead man's hand, with a lighted candle in it, believing in the superstitious notion that a candle placed in a dead man's hand will not be seen by any but those by whom it is used; and also, that if a candle in a dead hand by introduced into a house, it will prevent those who may be asleep from awaking. The inmates, however, were alarmed, and the robbers fled, leaving the hand behind them.*

In France, there is a later record of a 'Hand of Glory'. It was cut from the body of the murderer Lacenaire after his execution in Paris in 1836, and was possessed by the author Maxine du Camp.

There are several accounts of the 'Hand of Glory' being used during a burglary. Richard Harris Barham (1788-1845) mentions it in *The Ingoldsby Legend* and the Jesuit demonologist Del Rio recounts how a thief lit a 'Hand of Glory' before raiding a house, but was seen by a servant girl. The villains had not checked to see that everyone in the house was asleep before lighting the candle and speaking the incantation:

> *Let those who rest more deeply sleep,*
> *Let those awake their vigils keep;*
> *Oh Hand of Glory, shed thy light,*
> *And guide us to our spoils tonight.*

The incantation uttered meant that the servant girl would remain awake, so her task was to rouse the household. As the thief set about ransacking the house and disappeared into another room, the girl tried to extinguish the candle by throwing water, then beer over it and finally achieved success by using skimmed milk. The family awoke and the thief was caught.

William Henderson in his book on the subject relates a story that was originally collected by Charles Wastell from Bella Parkin, the daughter of the maidservant concerned. In the last decade of the eighteenth century, a traveller dressed as a woman came to the *Old Spital Inn*, near Stainmore, high on the Pennine hills of Yorkshire. She asked to stay the night, but refused a separate room, saying that she had to leave very early in the morning, and preferred to doze by the living-room fire. This was allowed, but the landlord told the servant girl in secret to sit up also until the stranger had gone.

After all had gone to bed, the maidservant lay down on the settle and, looking across at the supposed woman on the other side of the hearth, noticed a trouser-leg showing below the woman's skirt. With her suspicions now thoroughly aroused, she pretended to fall asleep, and saw the traveller take a 'Dead Hand' out of his pocket. He fixed a candle on it, lit it, and passed the whole thing several times before her face, saying, 'Let those who are asleep be asleep, and let those who are awake be awake.' He then put the 'Hand of Glory' on the table, and went to the house-door to whistle up his accomplices. The girl on seeing this jumped up immediately and pushed him through the door. Locking it behind him, and rushed upstairs to awaken her master. This, however, proved to be impossible. No amount of shouting, shaking or pulling would rouse him, or any other member of the family. Finally, as the thieves could still be heard prowling outside the house and might break in at any moment, she ran downstairs again, seized a bowl of skim milk, and emptied it over the 'Hand of Glory'. The flame went out, and thereafter she had no difficulty in waking the family.

In Louvain's, *Disquisitionum Magicarum*, published in 1599, the author describes a method of protecting a house against the 'Hand of Glory'. The householder must rub the threshold, or any part of the house by which thieves could enter, with an ointment made of the gall of a black cat, a white hen's fat, and the blood of a screech-owl. This ointment had to be prepared during the Dog-days (3 July - 11 August, when the Dog-star Sirius rises and sets with the sun). If it was properly made, and smeared in the right places, no 'Hand of Glory' brought into the dwelling would be effective.

As for the Danby 'Hand of Glory'. It is not known against whom this was used, nor in what manner it was applied. No records survive to tell us, but it remains as a fine specimen of a little known aspect of recent criminal folklore.

Chapter 11

A Miscellany of Murder

For some period a tollbooth was set up in Church Street by the abbot of Whitby Abbey for the collection of abbey dues. This tollbooth stood on or near the site of the present Tollbooth, often referred to as the Town Hall, that stands upon a colonnade of round pillars, and which was erected at the expense of Nathaniel Cholmley in the year 1788 (Figure 49). Some years previous to this date, however, on 10 December 1710, a puppet show was being presented to the townspeople for entertainment, when an affray was raised by a man named William Smith, who insisted on coming in without paying. It was then that the master of the puppet show drew his sword, and stabbed to death an innocent man called William Pickering during the ensuing tussle with Smith.

Afterwards, for this murder, the showman was apprehended and sent to York Castle, tried and convicted at the following Assizes, and executed. This incident was later utilised by the novelist Elizabeth Gaskell (1810-65) in her book *Sylvia's Lovers* to provide the culminating tragedy of her story.

On Monday, 3 April 1769, Valentine Bailey was executed at York for shooting at and murdering Mr John Smith, of Scarborough, Excise Officer, while going about his duty. On the jury returning a verdict of guilty, Bailey knocked down a woman who stood near him

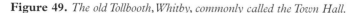

Figure 49. *The old Tollbooth, Whitby, commonly called the Town Hall.*

Figure 50. *Scarborough, South Sands, about 1800.*

in the dock, with whom he had been concerned in smuggling goods, and who was the principal witness against him. He died penitent, acknowledging the justice of his sentence, and his body was sent to the hospital for dissection.[22]

A circumstance occurred at Scarborough in the year 1804, which caused a considerable sensation at the time, and for many years afterwards was enveloped in mystery. A Miss Bell, daughter of a respectable confectioner, from York, while on a visit to Scarborough, was one morning found dead on the South Sands (Figure 50). The York Volunteers were at that time quartered at Scarborough Castle, and a young officer belonging to the corps was known to have been keeping company with the young lady, though it was against the

Figure 51. *A soldier at Scarborough Barracks, one of the many regiments which have been stationed here throughout the eighteenth and nineteenth centuries.*

wishes of her parents (Figure 51).

In consequence of this, and to break off the connection of the lovers, she was kept in confinement to her room, but the young woman managed to prevail upon a neighbour to let her out occasionally by the back way. While taking a walk one evening, it was thought she had been induced to accompany a man named Val Nicholson, along the Cayton road. Along here he was supposed to have murdered Miss Bell by strangulation, and then thrown the body over the cliffs, where it was found next day on the Sands at low water.

The young officer being also suspected of causing her death, was taken into custody and tried for murder, but no evidence was produced to convict him of the foul transaction, though the man Nicholson, and three others, named William Short, Jonathan Simpson, and Robert Johnson, falsely swore to have seen the officer with the young lady that night, in order to clear Nicholson of any blame. The evidence of a woman named Nelly Smailes was also given at the trial.

The soldier was acquitted of the charge; and all the men who

Figure 52. *The grave in St Mary's churchyard, Whitby, of a nine year-old child murdered in 1801.*

swore against him in subsequent years came to untimely deaths. The man Nicholson is said to have been more than once in a state of delirium, and while raving in one of these fits, he fancied he saw the young lady moving in front of him, calling upon his wife to look at her and take her away.

On his deathbed, however, Nicholson is reported to have eased his troubled conscience by confessing to have committed the murder of Miss Bell himself. The event was made the subject of a poem at the time, which had a wide circulation.[23]

Similarly, in the graveyard of St Mary's church, perched on the headland above the harbour of Whitby, is a small stone in the pathway beneath the window of the south transept (Figure 52). This small stone covers the remains of an innocent child of nine years old named Hubbersty who was cruelly murdered when he was deliberately pushed off the pier below and drowned in 1809. This act of unlawful killing, however, was not discovered until long after, when the *auctor sceleris* died some time later and confessed in a fit of remorse on his deathbed.

At Eskgateside, in the parish of Eskdale-cum-Ugglebarnby, stands a solidly built farmhouse of pleasing design named Birtley Farm, and having over the door the well-carved date 1697. It was here, on 14 September 1841, that the brutal murder of the farmer's wife, Mrs Robinson, took place in the kitchen while the men-folk were out in the fields getting in the harvest. This Mrs Robinson was the daughter of John Thistle, of Eskdalegates Farm, who was the grandson of Richard Chapman, of Lowdale in the same parish.

This violent event took place during the week, and so shocked the neighbourhood that on his return from nearby Whitby on the

Figure 53. *The old Georgian church at Sleights replaced on the same site by the present edifice.*

Saturday evening, the curate of Sleights Church sat down and wrote a sermon (Figure 53). In this he vividly described how,

> on Tuesday morning last, an unoffending female rose from her bed in good health and joyous spirits, and ere the sun had reached the meridian, she lay weltering in her blood – the victim of some ruthless ruffian, who, alas, has escaped detection!

For days the local Constabulary searched for Mrs Robinson's killer to no avail. Eventually, on the suggestion of the Marquis of Normandy, of nearby Mulgrave Castle, the Whitby Magistrates sought the assistance of the Metropolitan Police. In due course the Scotland Yard detectives proved that the crime had been committed by a labourer from county Durham, who had since died of smallpox at Shildon in that county. The labourer it was established had formerly been in the service of the farmer, Mr Robinson, and after the brutal killing had stolen a number of gold sovereigns from the parlour closet, thirty-one of which at least, he had spent before his death.

At some unspecified date, not far away from Birtley Farm, once stood the *Slip Inn*, which later became 'The Kennels' on Eskdaleside. During the nineteenth century in the days when it was still the *Slip Inn* it was frequented by hawkers' or pedlars' who roamed the countryside from village to village selling tea - the equivalent of the 'Rington's Tea' salesman of today. One particular pedlar was in the inn on a night when a fight broke out and was killed in the ensuing affray. It is not known whether this pedlar was involved in the fight, began it, or was an innocent bystander. Notwithstanding, it is said that his body was carried a short distance along the road to Blackbord Slack where there is a steep precipice down to the river and railway, here he was thrown over to be discovered some time later.

Chapter 12

The Body in the Bush –
Susannah Wilson, An Eighteenth Century Victim

The tiny village of Mickleby lies off the coast road between Whitby and Staithes before going on to Guisborough. Still very much an isolated agricultural community, in the eighteenth century its prospects must have been all the more rural. During the mid-eighteenth century, John Robinson owned much of the land in the area of Mickleby. He was thirty-three years of age at that time, a hard-working farmer, and happily married with a wife and four children. His affluence and business acumen allowed him to spend as much time as he deemed necessary with his family whom he appeared to adore. His wealth and position as one of the main employers in the district also afforded him a great respect within the local community. He was noted for his charitable acts toward the poor and homeless and was often seen to provide food from his land for any unfortunate souls who cared to call at his door. Those in his employment never went short nor was he a hard task-master and he was well thought of by his employees. In short his life seemed idyllic and his standing in the area assured. But all this was to change with the departure of the household maid, Susannah Wilson who left her position under mysterious circumstances.

Wilson had been a very efficient and highly respected maidservant in the Robinson household. Her sudden departure therefore came as a great shock to Mrs Robinson, who Susannah told of her leaving only hours before she actually went. Mrs Robinson, was naturally put out at the loss of such a good servant, but Wilson could not be persuaded to remain and in the end she left. Later, on reflection, Mrs Robinson began to suspect the true and much more sinister reason for Wilson's sudden departure than she had probably been given by the girl herself. Her husband refused to discuss the matter in any depth with his wife, nor allay his wife's suspicion of infidelity, and immediately set about employing another maidservant.

Elsewhere about the village, however, gossip was rife as to Susannah Wilson's sudden and unexpected departure. In the inns and taverns there was much speculation about the sexual relationship between master and maid which no one had believed at the time. Suddenly, however, it all began to fit together, and

Figure 54. *Bow Street, Guisborough in 1909, showing the old time-piece in the square which still stands.*

undoubtedly many believed the maidservant pregnant and had left in order not to incur the wrath of the father John Robinson who would no doubt have suffered if the fact had become known.

Susannah Wilson, meanwhile, had taken up temporary residence with friends at Guisborough (Figure 54). It was about twelve miles from there to Mickleby. During the interval she had kept contact with John Robinson for a meeting was arranged between them, and one spring morning Susannah set out for the meeting. She told friends that Robinson had promised her a bushel of wheat and she was going to collect it. But she also informed them of fears for her safety and said that if anything happened to her, or she should suffer any injury, then John Robinson should be the principal subject of an investigation despite his apparent outward show of respectability.

It was about twelve miles from Guisborough to Mickleby and Wilson did not seem too concerned about the distance as she set out to walk the journey. At Mickleby meanwhile, John Robinson performed his normal daily tasks and then late in the afternoon he informed the household that he was going to Staithes and would spend the night there with friends. He set out about five o'clock with every pretence of normality. At around seven o'clock that evening, the two met at their pre-arranged destination. The couple walked together and discussed their situation which probably centred around her ensuing pregnancy. Certainly John had more to fear than Susannah and one might feel that she could justifiably blackmail him and no doubt the farmer had this at the back of his mind as a prelude to his next act.

John Robinson wilfully led the former maidservant to an area that he had previously visited, an area which was perfectly suited for murder! Sitting down he lulled the girl into a false sense of security and made an excuse to leave her for a few moments. During this time he collected an axe which he had hidden at that location for precisely this reason. Creeping up on the unsuspecting maidservant with one swift blow of the weapon he split open her skull causing immediate death. Not content with that, in a frenzied attack he continued to beat Susannah Wilson's corpse with the axe until it was barely recognisable, his temper and relief so great.

Having gained control of his emotions, Robinson suddenly realised the consequence of his actions and was thus confronted with the immediate necessity of disposing of the body. A thick gorse bush close to the scene seemed the ideal hiding-place as the area was secluded and it appeared unlikely that anyone would ever have cause to visit. So the remains of Susannah Wilson were left to decompose in the inclement spring weather. Following this, in order to substantiate his alibi, Robinson then proceeded to Staithes where he arrived about half past nine o'clock. He remained the night with friends and returned to his farm and wife and children the following morning.

It was not for some five weeks, however, before rumours of Susannah Wilson's disappearance began to emerge. Having heard nothing for some time, her friends at Guisborough were concerned as to her welfare as they had not had word from the girl since she left for Mickleby. Recalling Wilson's own fears, enquiries were made with John Robinson and his household, but the farmer denied ever having arranged a meeting with the maidservant and promptly produced his alibi of having stayed at Staithes. His word was believed. It seemed inconceivable that Robinson should have had need to meet the girl again and no motive sprang to mind why he should have. There was further discussion among Wilson's friends and the authorities, and it

Figure 55. *A hanged man on the gibbet, once a common sight in the English countryside.*

was surmised that she might have gone elsewhere, moved on completely from the district, especially if she was pregnant. As it stood, however, it was nothing but conjecture that Robinson was her lover and that he had done away with Susannah to protect his reputation. Nevertheless, there were inconsistencies and the authorities returned to John Robinson with a request to search his entire property in case Wilson had suffered a fatal accident while trying to contact him. The farmer had no alternative but to grant such a request. Dozens of local people, including the male members of his own family participated in the search which took several hours to complete and concluded when news spread that a body had been found in a gorse bush in a remote field.

Initially the body was difficult to identify due to its advanced state of decomposition. None of the immediate searchers recognised any of the clothing of effects. But within minutes of being viewed by the friends from Guisborough, the body was named as that of Susannah Wilson.

Robinson came under immediate suspicion and was arrested. He was taken to York Castle where he later confessed to the crime. Following a trial, John Robinson was hanged for the murder of the girl Susannah Wilson (Figure 55). After death, his remains were later given to local surgeons for the purpose of dissection.

Chapter 13

A Smuggler's Revenge
~The Murder of James Law

Salt Pans is little more than an indentation on the East Coast of North Yorkshire some five miles north of Scarborough (Figure 56). It is about one mile from the village of Cloughton, to the north of Cloughton Wyke, on the rocky coast. On the night of Sunday, 20 August 1820, a lugger from Flushing, in Holland, successfully rendezvoused with the local smugglers and landed about two hundred tubs of gin and a quantity of tea and tobacco.

The smugglers may have been observed. The Revenue Officers were later to produce informants, who claimed to have witnessed the landing and to have recognised some of the smugglers involved, as the goods were carried away from the landing area. The following day the authorities were able to seize 115 tubs of gin, which were still concealed among the rocks, and attempted 'to rescue' a youth who was found guarding them. Not surprising the boy seems to have preferred not to wait until rescue arrived. A tub, or anker, held about eight and a half gallons of spirit, so the seize represented just under one thousand gallons of gin, but none of the smugglers were caught in the act.

Figure 56. *Salt Pans, near Scarborough.* Peter Howarth

Figure 57. *A revenue cutter chasing smugglers off the Yorkshire coast.*

In a tight, close-knit community such as the fishing community of Scarborough, virtually confined to a handful of crowded streets, the identity of the smugglers and their supporters could not be kept a secret for long, but that did not make the task of the Revenue Officers an easy one. Smuggling was widespread at that date and widely accepted (Figure 57). High rates of tax on imports, cumbersome regulations on trade practises and a high demand for the goods themselves, all encouraged smuggling and ensured that it was a popular and profitable enterprise, supported by many in all ranks of society.

In the face of such support, gathering evidence against the smugglers and persuading witnesses to stand up in court and give evidence, was a daunting task for the Revenue Service. The authorities were heavily dependent upon informers. The rate of payment to these persons was anything from twenty to fifty pounds, but in addition, the Revenue Officers took care to look after their informants in a variety of other ways. Such methods were proving very successful in the Scarborough district in 1820. The *Hull Advertiser* when reporting the Salt Pans landing noted that a great number of smugglers in the neighbourhood had been convicted lately, with heavy penalties. However, just as the identity of the smugglers was common knowledge to many, so people had a shrewd idea of who were the informants. William Mead, of Burniston, was widely believed to be the leader of a group that regularly supplied information to the authorities at Scarborough.

In the aftermath of the Salt Pans landing, Mead informed the Revenue Officers that he had been present at the place at about eleven o'clock that night. He had seen James Law and his son-in-law, John Scott, lead three horses loaded with twenty-one half-ankers of gin and two bales of tobacco from the beach. No less than eight other informants came forward to confirm this and name others involved. If they were all telling the truth, the little cove of Salt Pans must have been a crowded venue that August night.

The Revenue Officers, acting on the information received, arrested James Law and the others named, with the exception of John Scott, who fled when the Officers came to take him. The Attorney-General filed 'an information' against six individuals on smuggling charges; cases which were tried at the Exchequer in London, a court far removed from local interests and sympathetic juries. Mead and the other informants gave their evidence at the trials and all the smugglers were found guilty, except James Law who was acquitted.

It was this acquittal that was to spark off a train of events over three years, which was to involve hundreds of persons rioting in the streets of Scarborough, lead to several trials and was to culminate in the longest Assize case at York that anyone could ever recall following the murder of James Law in 1823.

Law was described as a respectable farmer who lived at Staintondale, just north of Cloughton. He was according to one girl, 'not an old man, nor a young one'. She thought he might not be sixty years of age. He had been convicted of smuggling in 1818 and was regularly found in the company of other known smugglers. His actions following the acquittal were obviously based on a desire for revenge. Yet whether it was because James Law was genuinely innocent in this instance and had been 'fitted-up' by Mead, or whether his acquittal provided the opportunity for the smugglers to try and reduce Mead's influence and activities against the gang, cannot be known. Either way, his response was to present eighteen indictments for perjury against William Mead and others who had given evidence at his trial. The Grand Jury at the Quarter Sessions decided that there was a case to answer and the matter was transferred to the Court of King's Bench.

Law's move was a bold one. As the trials would be held in London, Law and his supporters would be faced with the expense of taking their witnesses to the capital for several days, as well as meeting the legal costs of a series of trials. It was later to be claimed that the costs came to £5,000. Much of this was raised before the trials by public subscription in the Scarborough area, a further sign of the town's support and, perhaps, a pointer that Law was not acting alone. The first perjury case against William Mead came before the court in December 1822.

James Law was not the only person seeking revenge on the informants. In a case that was intertwined with that of Law, John Dodsworth, a farmer from Harwood Dale in Hackness, claimed that two men, Thomas Scott and William Bradbury, had broken into his dairy in November 1821 and stolen three butter firkins. They had sold them to Jonathan Bailey for three pounds. Both Scott and Bailey had been prosecution witnesses at the smugglers' trial in the previous year. Dodsworth had not brought any charges until August 1822, because Bradbury had been imprisoned in York Castle until that date (Figure 58). When released, he had confessed to Dodsworth and implicated Scott and Bailey in the robbery. He was to be the main prosecution witness.

When the case finally came to court in March 1823, it was to last a whole day, an unusual length of time for that period in history. Dodsworth was cross-examined for over two hours by defence counsel. He had to admit that he was soon to face smuggling charges and that he had been in London to give evidence against William Mead in the perjury trials and that Scott had been there on the other side. He was then asked if he did not expect Scott to be a witness against him in the forthcoming Exchequer trial. 'The question was put to him nearly a hundred times and in various forms, but he contrived to elude it, by fencing most ingeniously and it was not until his Lordship seriously admonished him on the consequences of prevarication that he directly stated that he knew Scott to be a witness for the Crown'.

The key witness for the prosecution was William Bradbury. He had spent time in the Houses of Correction at Beverley and Northallerton and two periods in York Castle. His evidence was that Scott had approached him to rob the farmer Dodsworth and that Bailey had agreed to buy the stolen goods from them. On being released from prison Bradbury said that he felt compelled to confess his part. Both he and Dodsworth were closely cross-examined over payments should Scott be convicted. Dodsworth denied making any promises to Bradbury and the defence failed to show that money he had been given whilst in prison was from Dodsworth.

Scott's defence was that the prosecution had been brought out of spite and malice and because he had given evidence against the smugglers. The constable of Whitby testified that on the slow journey

Figure 58. *The impressive York Castle goal (right of Cliffords Tower) with the York Assize building in the foreground.*

to York Castle to await trial, the two prisoners had argued most of the way. Scott had reproached Bradbury for swearing falsely against him and was told that if he had not testified in London, Bradbury would not have informed against him.

The Judge's summing-up left little room for misinterpretation. He pointed out the equivocation, contradictions and inconsistent conduct of many of the witnesses for the prosecution. This might well be a conspiracy to injure the prisoners. Against Jonathan Bailey, in his opinion, there was no satisfactory evidence and he left it to the jury to say, under all the circumstances, whether the proof against Scott was sufficiently conclusive.

The jury just took forty-five minutes to acquit Bailey and find Scott guilty. The Judge 'received the verdict with surprise and told the jury it was a very different one from what the evidence had led him to expect'.

That verdict in March 1823 can, perhaps, only be understood against events that go back to the perjury trials in December of the previous year and before. It had taken an hour to empanel a jury to try the unfortunate Scott, but it would appear improbable that the jury was not influenced by the background to the trial and was not caught up in the general excitement of events in Scarborough at that period.

There were over one hundred partisan Yorkshiremen in London in December 1822 in support of the parties at the perjury trials, the first of which centred on William Mead's evidence against James Law. Mr Jones, who had defended Law in the original smuggling trial, now led for the prosecution, 'an exception to the usual habits of his professional life.' He was instructed by the Scarborough solicitor, Mr Page, who appears to have been the preferred choice of smugglers in the district. Against them as Jones was to point out, was 'all the power of the Crown seemed put forth to protect the defendant'. Leading the formidable array of counsel on the opposing side were the Attorney-General and the Solicitor-General. The case was tried before Lord Chief Justice Abbot, and all-in-all the scene must have been a daunting one for many of the witnesses.

The basis of the case against Mead was that Law, who lived quite near to Salt Pans, had been away from home at the time of the landings. The informants had used this knowledge to concoct a story against him and Scott, his son-in-law. Jones then proceeded to outline Law's movements on the night. He had, as usual for Sunday, been to chapel and had ridden back as far as Scalby with the vicar. He had then called at another house to drink tea with friends until ten o'clock at night, before returning to his own home with two further acquaintances. Together they had prepared a cartload of wool, which he was taking to Pickering. He produced a succession of witnesses to confirm these events.

Scott, who denied having run away to avoid arrest, had been ill on that night in August 1820, and had gone to bed early. His wife could confirm this, but she could not at that time leave their young children to travel to London to give evidence.

The Solicitor-General for Mead, argued that the account of events was largely irrelevant. There was no need to dispute the visit to church, nor that Law had been drinking tea afterwards, but the house where he had been at ten o'clock was very close to Salt Pans and new witnesses had been discovered since the trial, who could confirm the presence of Law and Scott at the landing.

The Lord Chief Justice confirmed what was obvious to all. 'It was painful for him to say, that on one side or the other, there must have been very wilful and abundant perjury.' He left it to the jury to say which side was lying. After deliberating for two hours, the jury reached the conclusion that William Mead was guilty of perjury.

Law's triumph was short lived. If the supply of information against the smugglers was not to dry up, Mead had to be protected. The following day, Friday 20 December, when the second charge of perjury against Mead came before the court, the defence applied for a Special Jury. This entailed empanelling a jury formed from persons with a higher property qualification than the normal jury, in essence, jurors with a higher social standing. Court officials kept lists of special jurors, who were financially retained to attend the courts and serve as necessary.

When the names of the Special Jury were called, only five answered. This was not an uncommon event and was normally answered by a legal procedure known as 'praying a tales'; that is to move for a writ to summon sufficient additional jurors to make up the full number. It was usually a mere formality. When the Lord Chief Justice asked the defence, having asked for a Special Jury, to 'Pray a Tales', the Solicitor-General declined to do so. Jones, for the prosecution, protested bitterly. 'As he had not the Attorney-General's warrant,' (again normally a formality) 'he could not pray a tales'. To postpone the trials after Law had incurred considerable costs of nearly £5,000, would result in great hardship. He urged the Judge to force the defence to pray a tales and thus proceed with the trial. Abbot refused to do so. 'He had no power to force a defendant to pray a tales, or go to trial against their own judgement.' When the defence lawyers continued to refuse, the cases were put off until the next legal term.

James Law had every reason to feel bitter. If he felt he had been framed in his original trial, he had every justification for feeling that he had been unfairly treated in the capital. It was unlikely that the money to bring the prosecution witnesses to London and to meet the legal costs involved, could ever be raised again. Even if he pursued the case, there was no guarantee that the same strategy would not be employed against him a second time, for there was the distinct suspicion that steps had been taken to ensure that the Special Jurymen had not been available. As we shall see Law was not alone in his suspicions. To all intents and purposes, the perjury cases were at an end and the defendants would go free.

If Law felt that this was the worst that could happen, he was in for a further shock. Following the 'extraordinary exercise of discretional power by the law officers of the Crown',[24] in preventing Mead and his fellow informants coming to trial, the Solicitor-General moved for a new trial in the case where Mead had been found guilty of perjury. He asked that the verdict be set aside on two grounds. One, the jury's verdict had been against the weight of evidence, and secondly, that he had newly sworn affidavits to support Mead. One was made by a witness who had bought several tubs of spirits from Law on the night of the landing and a second was by a Pickering man, who had been told by James Law that he had been on a run the night before. After listening to the arguments, Lord Chief Justice Abbot granted a new trial and Mead was released to return to his home at Burniston on bail of £500 in his own name and two other sureties of £250. Law had every justification for feeling that he had been 'stitched-up!'

The case received much attention. *The Times*, an anti-government newspaper at this date, felt 'it almost exceeds credibility' that the officers of the Crown should 'both move for the special jury and refuse the tales'. It believed it was the first time since the 1688 Revolution that such an event had taken place, 'thus depriving the injured person of all power to bring his injuries before a court of justice'. It also raised the question of the cost of trials. 'Why is the country to fee a Counsel for the men prosecuted... in these cases? Above all, why is the country to fee such a phalanx of lawyers? There are five barristers employed in each of the eighteen cases.'

These criticisms were linked to a fierce attack on the special jury system, which allowed large numbers 'to live very comfortably and happily upon their trade and calling of special jurymen'. Once on the list and retained at five or six guineas a week, 'these men will naturally be inclined to a verdict for the Crown. These people are well known to the officers of the court, who select the jury... I fancy they are known to the judge, between whom and themselves that sort of intimacy grows, which disposes them to listen to his lordship's dictations and constructions with great complacency.' Such criticisms began to have political overtones. The *York Courant*, perhaps the paper with the widest circulation in Yorkshire, reprinted these views with approval.[25]

If the reaction to the perjury cases was one of surprise in London, it was one of outright fury in Scarborough. An effigy of Lord Chief Justice Abbot, dressed in a gown, was carried through the streets and burnt, whilst the shutters of Mead's house at Burniston were broken and split open. On 26 January 1823, the authorities dispatched a troop of the 2nd Dragoons (The Queen's Bays) from York to Whitby to assist the Revenue Officers. A second troop was sent to Scarborough. It is probable that this reflected the concern of the local Revenue Officers, who were undoubtedly facing open hostility. Coulson, the Whitby Collector, supplied William Mead with a brace of pistols with which to defend himself.

The anger did not die down quickly and was to reach an ugly climax on Thursday, 13 February. Thursday was market day in Scarborough, and on that date, John Dobson, a woodman from nearby Gowland was in town (Figure 59). He had spent the morning at the house of Maw, the Scarborough Revenue Officer, and then

Figure 59. *Newborough Bar, Scarborough, in the early nineteenth century. Criminals were often hung from this.*

gone on to the *Globe Inn*. He was later to deny that he had ever had
subsistence money from Maw, or that he had told the landlord at the
Globe Inn that Maw would pay his bill, but he had accepted that he
personally had not paid it and that he did not know who had.

When Dobson left the *Globe Inn* at 1.30 pm in the afternoon, he
unfortunately met James Law and a group of supporters coming
from the *Talbot Inn*. Dobson gave evidence that Law had told him
that if 'my friend Mead [was] along with me, we should neither of us
go home alive'. It was then that John Dobson was kicked to the
ground and dragged in all directions. One of the group, John Watson,
a convicted smuggler, urged, 'Damn him, kill him. He's an informing
rascal.' Law, no doubt expressing the frustration he had felt since
London, was reported to have said, 'It is no use prosecuting the
Crown's evidence; we will give them the club law at home'.

The unfortunate Dobson was knocked about for an hour then
taken to a pump where he was placed in the trough and had water
poured on him, whilst others threw all manner of filth at him and
beat him with a stick or whip. Soaked to the skin on a freezing
February day, Dobson came round from semi-consciousness to find
himself bound hand and foot to a ladder, which was being carried
through the streets. Not surprisingly, he could recollect little of the
afternoon's events, but he believed the mob were taking him 'down
to the sea to drown me'. He was rescued by men who found him
covered in blood that was running down his face. Anne Dawson, a
girl who had once worked for Mead as a servant, went to Burniston
and told him of Dobson's treatment at the hands of the smugglers.

James Law and John Dodsworth, the Harwood Dale farmer, were
in the *Talbot Inn* from six o'clock in the evening until after midnight.
Dodsworth was later to claim that 'I had got a little liquor [in me],
but I was not fresh', but it is probably significant that when they
came to ride home, Mrs Hutchinson, the landlady of the *Talbot Inn*,
sent John Watson to accompany them. He rode behind William
Hineson, Dodsworth's servant, as the four men travelled northwards
out of Scarborough on a direct road which took them past William
Mead's house in Burniston.

It was 2.00 am before they reached that point. The quartet denied
calling at Slightholme Robinson's alehouse, but witnesses in the
village claimed that they had been awakened by a great racket and
that the men were there for twenty minutes, calling the publican up
in a very rough manner, before they moved further up the road to
Adam Calvert's inn, to demand 'some more drink'. Not surprisingly,
Calvert 'would not get up'. By this time many persons along the road

Figure 60. *A corner of Burniston village on what is now the main Scarborough-Whitby road.*

had been awakened and lay listening to the men and horses, as they made their way through the village.

William Mead's house, a shop, lay at the top of Burniston village (Figure 60). It was fronted by a pavement some two or three feet wide, and raised about three feet above the roadway. It was later to be argued whether a horse could have mounted the raised causeway at that point. Mead, his wife, and eleven-year-old daughter Dorothy lay in one bed in the upstairs room. A friend, Robert Belt, was asleep in another bed in the same room. Next door, separated from them by only a thin and holed partition, dividing what had once been one house, lay Elizabeth Jennison and her mother, sharing a bed because Mrs Jennison's husband was away.

They were all awakened by the noise from the four smugglers as they stopped beneath Mead's window. Amid the shouting, John Watson began to sing 'a party song', one of triumph concerning William Mead's perjuries and his conviction. After about three or four minutes, Elizabeth Jennison said she heard the sound of breaking glass from next door and the noise of gunfire. It transpired that Mead had shot at James Law who was hit in the shoulder, and the ball travelling down lodged in his chest. Law was taken to Dodsworth's house at Harwood Dale and died there a week later on 24 February 1823.

In the aftermath of the shooting, two of Mead's neighbours, a father and son, Thomas and George Brown, left Burniston with Robert Belt. They all reached the house of Mead's brother at

Staintondale about 5.00am, on their way to Whitby. The youngster, George Brown, was to prove an important witness at the subsequent trial of William Mead. Mead appears to have acted with great coolness following the shooting, going back to bed and claiming not to have heard the pounding of the Scarborough constable on his door until it was broken open with a sledge-hammer. He offered no resistance, willingly produced the brace of pistols and allowed himself to be taken off in handcuffs, along with his wife and daughter, to Scarborough, where he was confined in irons in the Poor House there.

News of the incident quickly spread through the town and surrounding countryside, helped by John Watson, who walked through Scarborough wearing Law's top coat, complete with bullet hole and blood. He wore it, he said at the trial, to keep himself warm as he had no coat of his own, but he agreed that he freely admitted it was the late James Law's and did not discourage anyone from examining the garment as he wandered about the streets.

The town was still at fever pitch on Saturday, 15 February when William Mead asked William Dawson to go to Burniston to collect a box and a trunk of his belongings and bring them back to Scarborough. Dawson was the father of Anne Dawson, the girl who had told Mead of the attack on Dobson in Scarborough. Indeed, Dawson had been deeply involved in events from the beginning. He had spent four or five weeks in London before the perjury trials, though he did not appear as a witness. 'Mr Maw [the Scarborough Revenue Officer] asked me to go and I went.' He thought he might have received seventy pounds in expenses for going. He kept a lodging house in Scarborough with his four daughters, though opposing counsel at the trial were to insinuate that it was a brothel.

Dawson hired a porter called Tindall to drive a cart to Burniston for Mead's belongings. As the two men returned to Scarborough, they were stopped by John Watson and two other men on horseback. Watson was furious with Dawson and made threats. Having then made his point, he turned and with his companions rode into Scarborough for assistance, crying that 'they had got another rebel!' William Dawson, well aware of what had happened to Dobson, ran from the cart and tried to make his escape across the fields, but was soon chased by a mob of over two hundred, who caught up with him, dragged back over the fields and then along the road into town, pelting him with stones and mud all the while. Dawson was finally rescued by one of the town officers, but took eight days to recover from his injuries. It is said that Grace Dawson, a daughter, did not

CUSTOM HOUSE, LONDON,
10th March, 1823.

WHEREAS it has been represented to the Commissioners of His Majesty's Customs, that a number of Persons have at various times, in the course of the Month of February last, and the present Month of March, assembled themselves riotously and tumultuously about the House of ROBERT MAW, an Officer of the Customs, at the Port of *Scarborough*, situate in *Scarborough* in the County of *York*, particularly on the Night of Saturday the 15th ultimo, when the Rioters broke his Windows, and made every possible effort to gain an entrance into his Dwelling-house, with intent to do him and his Family some bodily Harm:

The said Commissioners are hereby pleased, in order to bring to justice the Persons who have been guilty of the said Outrage, to offer a Reward of

ONE HUNDRED POUNDS

To any Person or Persons who shall discover or cause to be discovered any one or more of the Persons actually concerned therein, to be paid on Conviction, by the Collector of His Majesty's Customs, at the Port of *Scarborough*.

By Order of the Commissioners,
G. DELAVAUD, Sec.

CUSTOM HOUSE LONDON,
10th March, 1823.

WHEREAS it has been represented to the Commissioners of His Majesty's Customs, that a violent Outrage was committed on the Person of WILLIAM DAWSON, of *Scarborough*, in the County of *York*, Farmer, on the 15th ultimo, near *High Peasholm*, by a number of Persons riotously assembled about him, some of whom seized him by the Collar, threw Dirt and Stones at him, kicked him over his body, legs, and thighs in a most inhuman manner, and then dragged him into *Tanner Street* in *Scarborough*, where they threw large Stones at him, which knocked him down, and by which, his Head, Nose, and right Eye were dreadfully injured, and the said WILLIAM DAWSON was placed in the most imminent danger of his life:

The said Commissioners are hereby pleased, in order to bring to justice the Persons who have been guilty of the said Outrage, to offer a Reward of

ONE HUNDRED POUNDS

To any Person or Persons who shall discover or cause to be discovered any one or more of the Persons who were actually concerned therein, to be paid upon Conviction, by the Collector of His Majesty's Customs, at the Port of *Scarborough*.

By Order of the Commissioners,
G. DELAVAUD, Sec.

Figure 61. *Reward notices posted after the Scarborough riots, 1823.*

Figure 62. *Scalby church and churchyard in which James Law is buried.*

Figure 63. *The old drawbridge, Whitby, which was later replaced by swing bridges.*

recognise her father when he was brought home.

There were other violent disturbances. The house of Maw, the Revenue Officer was stoned. There was a riot in Burniston and more violence in Scarborough that led the magistrates to swear in seventeen Special Constables, seven of them from the Preventive Service. The Commissioners of Customs posted rewards of one hundred pounds to be paid for information leading to the conviction of those involved,[26] but feelings continued to run high (Figure 61). The jury at the inquest of James Law returned a verdict of 'wilful murder' by Mead and Belt, whilst 1500 people attended Scalby Church to witness Law's burial and to hear the verses of the derogatory song about William Mead sung over the grave (Figure 62). When Mead and Belt were transferred to York Castle to await trial, they were given a military escort as far as Whitwell-on-the-Hill.

Those engaged in smuggling were quick to take advantage of the situation to cause confusion. Apart from the verses, which were printed up in Driffield and sold in Whitby and York, a broadsheet entitled 'On the late Barbarous Murder of Mr James Law by William Mead, the Government Hireling Murderer' was fixed to Whitby bridge and distributed throughout the district (Figure 63). Even before Law's death, a press handout had been prepared, which was then printed in the *York Courant*, the *Sheffield Independent*, the *York Herald, Leeds Independent, Hull Advertiser*, and the *Doncaster Gazette.*

The statement gave a long and very partisan view of events, and employed a flowery, melodramatic style of prose to paint a biased picture of premeditated murder. According to the statement, Mead formed 'diabolical intention' of taking Law's life as he returned from market. This 'atrocious resolve' was to 'satiate his horrid thirst for blood'. It alleged that Mr Law purposely delayed his journey until the early hours of the morning, 'judging by that time, the eye of malice would be closed', but 'William Mead, like a staunch murderer' had waited for his victim 'through the lonesome stillness of the night' and 'discharged the murderous ball'.

It was thought by many from the language and style of reporting that the author was Page, the solicitor acting for the prosecution against Mead.

The trial of Mead and Belt for the murder of James Law was scheduled to be heard at the same Yorkshire Lent Assizes as that which Scott was found guilty of the burglary at John Dodsworth's Harwood Dale farm. The latter case had been heard against the background of Law's death and the subsequent disturbances, which perhaps helps to explain a verdict that the presiding Judge clearly felt

was against the weight of evidence. It did not auger well for William
Mead and Robert Belt.

It is perhaps not surprising under these circumstances, that the
defence counsel did their utmost to delay the trial. On the opening
day, 18 March, they protested to the Judge that George Brown, who
was seen as a key witness by both sides, was being prevented from
attending. His father had sworn an affidavit that the boy was being
held against his will in a house at York. When he had gone to collect
his son, several people had seized the boy and forcibly detained him.
There had been a disturbance in the street involving the solicitor
Page, Haxby, the Burniston constable, and two people who had been
witnesses against Scott and Bailey. The defence asked for and
obtained a writ of *habeas corpus* to produce George Brown at the
trial, which was then delayed until 25 March 1823.

When the trial next began, Mr Williams for the defendants rose to
demand that the trial be postponed yet again because 'systematic
attempts had been made to poison the public mind and to prejudice
the opinions of the jury'. He read out the article from the newspapers
(mentioned previously), the verses about Mead's perjury and the
broadsheet, 'laying the greatest emphasis possible on the most
objectionable words'. He further produced a sworn affidavit that
prosecution witnesses arriving in York in two post-chaises, had
scattered copies of the verses as they had driven through the city
street. He 'was reliably informed' that Page was one of the passengers
in the chaises. He reminded the Judge that it had been necessary to
obtain a writ of *habeas corpus* to ensure that George Brown was free
to give evidence. The defence had been hindered in preparing its case
because of the deliberate slowness in returning the written
depositions of witnesses to the court and the defence solicitor had
been prevented from gaining access to Mead's house in Burniston by
Haxby the constable. Under these circumstances, he submitted that
William Mead and Robert Belt were not likely to receive a fair and
impartial trial.

Following William's opening speech the trial was adjourned until
the following day, mainly to allow Page time to answer the charge of
being involved at that level. In a sworn statement, he stated that he
did not know that the broadsheet had been distributed in York and
was not privy to such distribution. He had neither authorised,
directed or advised it. Both the defence counsel and the Judge noted
that Page had confined his denial solely to events in York.

Jones, the prosecuting counsel, objected to the postponement. He
argued that the jury was quite capable of ignoring the pamphlets. If

people were to be disqualified from serving as jurors because they had read an account of what had happened in a newspaper, no offender 'in these days of education' would be brought to trial. He suspected that the defence was simply trying to delay matters for as long as possible. The prosecution 'had no public purse to meet the costs, in contrast to the defence. By what good fortune the prisoner, who had been a witness for Government, had four counsel, his friend opposite might answer. If these proceedings were to be carried on, the effect would be the prisoners must escape, for no private prosecution could stand such warfare. He hoped the question was not a political one.'

The Judge ruled that witnesses who had chosen to come to York several days earlier than was necessary and who had distributed inflammatory publications in the assize town, could have done so only to improperly influence those people into whose hands they fell. Under all circumstances it was his duty to agree to the trial being postponed until the following assizes.

Having succeeded in their first objective of delaying the trial, the defence lawyers then applied for a writ of *certiorari* to remove the case from the Yorkshire Assizes to the court of the King's Bench in London. The Lord Chief Justice felt the Court was in a considerable difficulty. The publications the defence complained about were a grievous misconduct and one that might well prejudice a fair trial, but if the writ was granted the trial would certainly be delayed and might never take place. The prosecutors might not be able to face the costs of pursuing the case, bringing witnesses to London and maintaining them there. Under the circumstances it was right to refuse the application and the trial must be heard in Yorkshire (Figure 64).

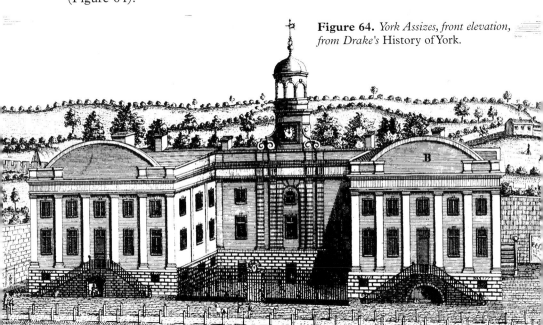

Figure 64. *York Assizes, front elevation, from Drake's* History of York.

Robert Belt is a somewhat shadowy figure in these events, a peaceable man in his early thirties, who kept a public house. Although he was a friend of Mead, he had played no part in earlier occurrences. He had arranged to spend the night of the shooting at Thomas Brown's house at Burniston and accompany him and his son to Whitby the following day, but, at the last moment, he had slept at Mead's house instead.

William Mead was thirty-six years of age, mild-mannered, 'tradesmanlike' and respectable looking, but with a confident air, even jaunty. He wore a rose in the buttonhole of his coat throughout the trial. He remained very composed, writing short notes to his counsel during the hearing and showing no anxiety when the jury was out. Belt was much more affected by the trial, but both men appeared to be in good spirits when they were brought into court on Monday, 21 July 1823.

The case was still causing considerable excitement and a large crowd assembled before six o'clock in the morning ready to be admitted at seven-thirty. The press interest was such that the Under Sheriff supplied the reporters with tickets and arranged for them to be let into the courtroom early. The gallery windows were removed in an attempt to get more air into the crowded room. It was nine o'clock before Mr Justice Holroyd took his seat, but it took a further hour to empanel the jury. All potential jurors from the East and North Ridings were excluded and sixty-six names were called before there was satisfaction. Finally at about ten o'clock Mr Jones rose for the prosecution to ask the jury 'not to make the case a political issue', but the pressure and disorder in the public galleries was such that it was several minutes before he could be heard.

Inevitably a greater part of the morning was spent outlining the events of James Law's return from Scarborough. Dodsworth, Watson and Hineson gave their version of the shooting and medical evidence was called about the nature of the wound and the cause of death. Witnesses testified to hearing the sound of breaking glass from Mead's window before the shot was fired and Jones showed that when the window was examined the glass had been broken from the inside. In one sense however, much of this evidence was secondary to the main question, for Mead neither denied breaking the window nor discharging the shot. The vital issue in the trial was whether he was justified in doing so. If his actions were not justified then the fact that he had fired the shot would not help the unfortunate Belt, for in law, if Belt had aided and abetted Mead, the question of who had actually pulled the trigger was immaterial. The act of one was the act of both and Robert Belt would be equally guilty of murder.

The defence was able to achieve a significant success in the cross-examination of John Watson. Despite an objection from the prosecution, the Judge ruled that Watson could be questioned about events in Scarborough on the day Law was shot. The defence was thus able to bring out details of the mob attack on John Dobson and, significantly, that Anne Dawson had told Mead what had happened in town. This was to prove the central issue of the trial. If Mead could show that he was genuinely apprehensive for his safety, then his actions could be defended and if he could show that his house was actually under attack, then the firing of the gun might even be justified. The way in which the defence was able to establish that Mead knew the way the smugglers had treated Dobson in Scarborough earlier that day was a strong point in his defence.

In this context, the causeway outside Mead's house was crucial to his defence. The jury were shown an accurate model of the scene made by the defence. It showed the raised causeway in front of the house measuring some two to three feet wide and three feet from the road surface, but broken in places, where, it was argued by the defence, horses could be ridden up to the house itself (Figure 65). If the smuggler's had simply sat on their horses in the middle of the street below Mead's window, taunting him by their singing and insults, such behaviour might be annoying, even frightening, but

Figure 65. *The shooting of James Law from Mead's house, Burniston, in 1823.*

would fall short of justifying his use of the pistol. If, on the other hand, they were actually on the causeway, banging on the door and windows in a manner which suggested that they were trying to force an entry, then Mead might successfully plead self-defence. Both sides were well aware of the importance of this issue and all the smugglers were closely cross-examined on the point, with the other witnesses removed from the courtroom. All denied alighting from their horses and were adamant that they had not ridden on to the causeway, nor hammered on the windows.

There were independent witnesses. The prosecution called Elizabeth Jennison, who had lain in bed with her mother listening to events. She was immediately next door to Mead, separated only by a thin partition, but without the benefit of a window overlooking the road. She heard Law's party, but there had been no attack on the house, no trampling on the causeway and no knocking on Mead's door and window. The defence tried to discredit her by showing that she was on bad terms with Mead's wife. She had been forced to leave the Methodist Church three years before because of an adulterous relationship with a married man. Mead's wife had 'made free with me with her tongue. She talked scandal about a man and me.' They also produced a witness who claimed to have overheard Elizabeth Jennison persuading Mead's young daughter, Dorothy, that she had not heard anything threatening on the night and that she would go to gaol if she said that she had. According to this witness, the eleven-year-old child had replied, 'Oh Betty, you must have heard the horses upon the causeway and did you not hear the knocking at the door?'

Neither Elizabeth Jennison for the prosecution, nor Mary Halliday, the defence witness called to undermined her story, were convincing witnesses and all really depended upon the evidence of George Brown. Described as 'a young boy' he was without obvious links to either party. George was the youth who had been held by the prosecution in York without his father's knowledge, in an apparent attempt to prevent him from giving evidence.

George Brown lived at Burniston with his father, close to the house of William Mead. On the night in question he had been up and about at two o'clock in the morning. He was excited and could not sleep because he was to set out at dawn with his father and Robert Belt to visit his sister at Lofthouse, beyond Whitby. Robert Belt had been expected to be sleeping in the Brown household and had stayed instead with Mead only at the last moment. The boy testified that soon after getting up and lighting a fire, he heard 'a noise like knocking at doors or windows'. He thought it was from Billy Mead's house, because 'they' [the smugglers] had been there a night or two before when it was it was the talk of the town that they had been breaking in the window shutters. He had opened the door of his house to look out. 'When I was at the door, I heard the noise as if of knocking. I thought it came from William Mead's door; after the second knocking, I heard the report of a gun or pistol instantly.' After the shooting Belt had come round and joined his father and they had all set out for Lofthouse as planned.

The prosecution case took up the whole of the first day until 6.30pm, when the Judge adjourned proceedings and placed the jury under the custody of a court bailiff for the night. They shared the Grand Jury Room where beds and refreshments were provided by the High Sheriff. The jury returned to the court at eight o'clock next morning, but it was not until nine o'clock that the Judge took his seat. The defence opened their case.

An important witness was John Dobson, who was taken through his experiences in Scarborough on the afternoon of Law's death. The defence established that Mead was fully aware of the way he had ben treated by Law and Dodsworth. They called Anne Dawson to testify that she had informed Mead of the events in Scarborough on the same day that they occurred. She was also able to confirm that George Brown had told her of the banging on William Mead's door when she had seen him at five o'clock in the morning at Staintondale, as the Browns and Robert Belt had rested on their way to Lofthouse. She admitted that because of her evidence she was now too frightened to return to Scarborough.

Mr Justice Holroyd summing-up lasted for nearly four hours. The key passages concentrated on the law of trespass. Civil trespass did not justify the firing of the pistol. If the jury was satisfied that James Law and his party had done nothing more than ride up to the house of Mead and sing songs, then no matter how offensive and irritating their actions were, that did not justify the assault on them. If there had been no attack on the house, no violence offered and there was no reasonable apprehension to expect an attack, then the death of Law was murder. However, a man's dwelling-house was his castle, his place of refuge. If this was invaded in the middle of the night, it was almost like an assault upon the person. If William Mead had reasonable grounds for believing that he and his family were in personal danger, then his actions might amount to manslaughter or might even be fully justified.

The jury took just twenty-five minutes to find William Mead guilty of manslaughter and to find Robert Belt not guilty. The Judge called it 'a most proper verdict on the evidence' and accepted that Law and the others had behaved 'in a very improper and outrageous manner'. Mead though, had shown that he did not have 'sufficient regard for the life of a fellow creature'. The Judge in his sentence however was inclined to leniency because Mead had already spent some considerable time in prison and must have suffered greatly because of what had happened on that night. His final verdict was that William Mead should spend two years in prison. The *York Courant* delayed publication that day in order to carry the account of the trial and verdict.

The case despite its conclusion continued to arouse political passions. The Tory newspaper in York, which had campaigned for William Mead's acquittal, was exultant that the murder charge had failed and attacked the Whig inclined *York Courant* for printing the first prejudiced account of Law's death. This, it argued, had aroused such animosity against Mead that it had been difficult to hold a fair trial. The *York Courant* defended its actions, complaining about a tirade of abuse in the Tory journal and talked darkly of preferring to see ten guilty men go free rather than one innocent man suffer. The guilty, it concluded, would one day face a higher Judge.

Other men however had still to face an earthly court. Numerous people had been arrested after the disorders in Scarborough and Burniston. Some like Watson and Scott were prominent smugglers, others were simply caught up in events and now faced trial for riot and assault. Others like Ben Topham had fled before they could be seized.

The first of these trials concerned the riots in Scarborough and the assault on John Dawson. After hearing the prosecution evidence, the Judge interrupted the defence counsel. 'I will tell you what my opinion is; that there was a violent ferment in the town of Scarborough and that in the midst of such ferment, persons acted under wrong feelings.' He gave a clear hint that if the defendants accepted the charges they would be dealt with leniently. The prosecution indicated that they would accept the defendants' own bond to keep the peace. On this basis, the remaining cases were dealt with quickly, but in one instance, passions still ran deep and were still sufficiently inflamed for the defendants to refuse to be bound over. The Crown decided not to proceed and the trial was stopped. In this decision it was seen that there was perhaps a general desire to see calm and peace restored to the town. This may have been an optimistic ideal, for before the defendants were dismissed, Mr Page, as always the solicitor for the smuggling fraternity, rose to complain

Figure 66. *Smugglers attacked - a popular and romanticised nineteenth century print by an unknown artist showing revenue men capturing smugglers.*

that the Crown witnesses had begun to insult those on the other side. It was more than likely that it would be some considerable time before the rival factions left Scarborough at peace.

In conclusion, an incident in the year 1817, three years before the smugglers landed their illicit cargo at Salt Pans, sheds an interesting light on William Mead's character. At that date although he was described as a considerable farmer at Stainton, he was in embarrassing circumstances. A writ was issued against him, presumably for debt, and in the normal way, the Sheriff issued a warrant for his arrest. The officer entrusted with carrying out the duty discovered that Mead was at his brother's house. It was also thought that Mead would resist arrest and so the officer set five men in hiding around the house to try and catch him in the open. He then took himself off to a nearby public house to await developments.

After lying in ambush for some time, the Sheriff's Officers saw the door cautiously opened, William Mead look around then start to cross the yard. As they moved to arrest him, unfortunately they were seen and Mead dashed back to the house but was grabbed in the act of trying to close the door (Figure 66). One of the five officers,

Joseph Trott, put his knee between the door and frame to prevent it fully closing. Mead, half-held through the gap, called for his brother to bring an axe and struck several blows with the cutting edge to Trott's knee, wounding him severely. The door was finally forced opened and both brothers arrested. They were charged with grievous bodily harm.

At the subsequent trial, their counsel, Mr Gilby, put up in their defence three legal objections to the prosecution case. Firstly, they had produced in court the warrant authorising the sheriff's officers to take Mead into custody, but failed to produce the writ on which the warrant was based. The Judge agreed that this should have been in court. Secondly, since the district of Pickering-cum-Lythe was a separate jurisdiction, the writ could not be executed at that place by the Sheriff's officers. A mandate should have been directed to the Chief Bailiff of the district commanding him to execute the warrant. Finally, Gilby's third argument was that the actions of the five assistants was illegal. They were not acting in the presence of the Sheriff's officer and aiding him in the execution of his duty as the officer was elsewhere in the public house.

The Judge agreed. There were too many legal objections for the case to proceed and he directed the jury to acquit the two brothers.[27]

In 1828 Mead approached various persons in the Leeds area claiming to be seeking the rightful heirs to inheritances unclaimed in Chancery. The *Leeds Intelligencer* reported that the number of Leeds people who were willing to hand over copies of wills, registers of baptisms and money to cover Mead's expenses 'exceeds belief'. Needless to say, William Mead then disappeared, but his obituary, sent through the post, appeared soon afterwards in a London newspaper. It was later reported that Mead had been seen in the towns of Goole and Hull.[28] By the year 1830 however, he was back in the Scarborough area (Figure 67).

In an interesting twist to his life, following his last criminal act in 1830, William Mead found himself once more in the dock at York Assizes in July of that year, charged with stealing two oxen and a heifer from a farmer named Stubbs who lived at Harwood Dale. The animals had been left grazing in a field two miles from the farm buildings, but had been removed by Mead during the night. At four-thirty in the morning he was observed driving them through Saltersgate 'by a man named Belt, who is ostler at an inn there'. Robert Belt, onetime friend of Mead, was to be the prime prosecution witnesses at York – an irony. Mead had then continued on to Malton, where he had employed a man to drive the beasts to

Figure 67. *William Mead's house, Burniston, as it is today.*

York, whilst he followed in comfort by carrier's wagon. The aggrieved owner had finally caught up with Mead at the *Wagon and Horses* near Walmgate Bar in York. The missing animals were found in the landlord's field nearby.

William Mead had nothing to say in his defence at the trial. The jury found him guilty and he was sentenced to death.[29]

Chapter 14

Doctor Death –
Edward William Pritchard (1825-65)

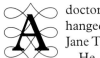 doctor of medicine, Edward William Pritchard was hanged in Glasgow in 1865 for poisoning his wife Mary Jane Taylor and mother-in-law among others he killed.

He was born on 6 December 1825 in Southsea, Hampshire, the son of a Royal Naval Captain, and educated exclusively for the medical profession at Portsmouth. He became an apprentice surgeon in the British Royal Navy in 1846, but resigned his post in 1851 at the age of twenty-six. He married Mary Taylor in 1850, the daughter of an Edinburgh silk-merchant. During their first year, Mary lived with her parents in Edinburgh while Pritchard served on HMS *Hectate*. However, his in-laws thought this an unsuitable arrangement, and they found Dr Pritchard a practice in Yorkshire which they persuaded him to take up. The couple settled in Hunmanby (Figure 68), Dr Pritchard as a general practitioner with a branch surgery in Filey and was appointed Medical Officer of No. 3 District of the Bridlington Union.

Figure 68. *Bridlington Street, Hunmanby.*

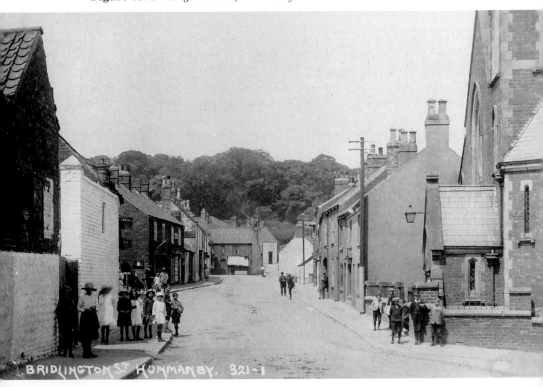

Figure 69. *The Crescent and Crescent Gardens c.1905.*

During the six years he and Mary Jane were at Hunmanby four children were born to them, Jane Frances, who was called Fanny; Charles, Horace and Kenneth. These children adored their father, and Edward could never resist admiration. They doted on him, and he doted on them; and of course, this was a great pleasure to Mary Jane. Later they lived at Filey, in Rutland Street, not far from the Crescent (Figure 69). However, during their residence in Yorkshire his wife often visited her parents in Edinburgh, which left the doctor alone and able to pursue various amorous affairs.

Dr Pritchard became a prominent Freemason and, being of a literary turn of mind, wrote on many subjects of local interest and published a small *Guide to Filey*. His eccentric habits, however, were a source of annoyance to the villagers of Hunmanby. Often when attending Church, he would arrange with his groom beforehand, to call him out midway through the vicar's sermon and so cause a deliberate commotion. When not at Church he still made his presence felt, however, by galloping on horseback up and down the Church Hill to the distraction of both priest and worshippers at service.

Other personal abhorations included his story-telling and womanising. This latter was to be his downfall at Filey. He enjoyed examining attractive young women and he found it stimulating to discover how far he could go in these little surgery flirtations. One day a very charming young woman visited his surgery and Edward was immediately excited by her presence. He, of course, could not resist trying it on. Unfortunately, he clearly misjudged this particular woman, for when she understood his intentions she protested vigorously, adding that she would return home immediately and inform her husband of his unprofessional conduct which caused Dr Pritchard some alarm.

His fears proved well-founded, for the next day, the woman's husband appeared at the surgery and demanded to see Edward. He was a man older than his wife, of choleric temper and clearly determined to have his revenge. He told Pritchard he was a scoundrel, and assured him that he would be hearing more of this disgraceful affair, and in time Edward learnt that there was to be a prosecution against him. Luckily, however, the husband of the woman he insulted, dropped down dead suddenly. In view of this she was not inclined to continue the case being in a state of shock!

The strain of the incident, however, effected Dr Pritchard's health. His wife's family, whom he managed to keep the scandal from, thought he had been working too hard with one practice in Hunmanby and another in Filey in addition to his writing and lecturing. The Taylor's therefore, were only too glad to have their daughter and grandchildren stay with them in Edinburgh whilst Edward took a post as Medical Attendant to a wealthy man who was travelling for his health. So, having bought a diploma of Doctor of Medicine in *absentia* from Erlangen University, Scotland in 1857, and becoming a Licentitate of the Society of Apothecaries in London, Dr Edward Pritchard left Filey and its environs and England and spent some months in Egypt and the Holy Land, later returning to Glasgow and a new practice within easy reach of his wife's family.

Although his notoriety was achieved while living elsewhere, local tradition avers that even while living and practising in the neighbourhood of Hunmanby and Filey, the good doctor was trying out the effects of various poisons upon his patients, as witness the case of old Betty Chandler. In this instance, the story goes, that one

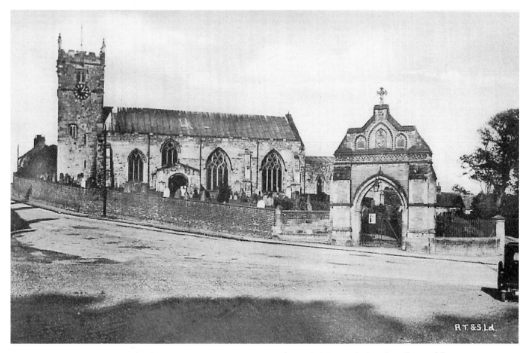

Figure 70. *All Saints' church, Hunmanby, in which is buried a daughter of Dr Edward Pritchard.*

day as Dr Pritchard was returning from a nearby village to Hunmanby, he heard the church bell tolling. On making enquiry, he was told of the death of Betty Chandler whom he had been treating for unspecified ailments. In response to the information of Betty's death, he put spurs to his horse and dashed to her cottage, whereupon it is said he hastily disposed of the medicine that he had supplied as a curative. This incident appeared of little account at the time, but was recalled to mind when some years after leaving the village, the extent of his nefarious deeds came to light.

It was also during his sojourn in Yorkshire, that his little daughter died, and while it was never suggested that Pritchard had a hand it, no one can rule out the possibility. She is buried in the churchyard of All Saints, Hunmanby (Figure 70).

Dr E W Pritchard was hanged on 28 July 1865, on Glasgow Green, and his was the last public execution in Scotland.

Chapter 15

The Babe in the Wood –
John William Pickering (d.1880)

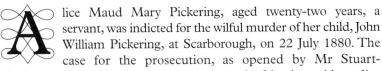

lice Maud Mary Pickering, aged twenty-two years, a servant, was indicted for the wilful murder of her child, John William Pickering, at Scarborough, on 22 July 1880. The case for the prosecution, as opened by Mr Stuart-Wortley, was that the prisoner was accused of having with malice aforethought killed her little boy, aged between two and three years of age on the night of the date in question. On 8 August the body of the child was found dead in a stream running to the sea a little distance outside the town of Scarborough (Figure 71). The last time the child had been seen alive was eight days previous, when it was being taken into a wood near the stream by its mother, Alice

Figure 71. *Peasholm Glen, Scarborough, with its little brook flowing through wooded landscape.*

Figure 72. *Seamer village, near Scarborough.*

Pickering. The prosecution was not able to show by eye-witness or forensic evidence what happened to the child in the wood, all that could be proved was that it was taken into the wood between seven and eight o'clock in the evening by the accused, and that when she was next seen that evening the child was not with her.

The prisoner was a married woman, and it is supposed that in her married life there were many circumstances which were not happy. She was married in November 1877. For twelve months afterwards, she and her husband lived together at the house of her husband's mother at Seamer, in the confines of Scarborough (Figure 72). The child was born in March 1878 and christened John William. Sometime after the child was born they went to live at Ayton. According to the prisoner's statement, she there left her husband on account of some ill-usage. They spent the next year or two sometimes living together and sometimes separate, while the child had spells living with the prisoner's mother.

In the spring of 1880 Alice Pickering was living separated from her husband with a woman named Jane Ellen Smith, in North Street, Scarborough, while the child resided with its grandmother. At that date the child was brought back to its mother. Some little time afterwards Alice asked Smith where it was likely that she could find some one to take charge of the child. Smith gave her the name of Mary Ann Major, who about June of 1880, undertook to nurse the child for the amount of 4s 6d per week. On the day that the child was taken to Major's residence, the prisoner left Smith's house to live elsewhere.

The next fact known concerning her was that on 26 June she came and visited Mrs Major and, on the pretext that she wanted to show the child to a lady from whom she expected to get a situation, took the child away. The child was not brought back to Mrs Major, and the 4s 6d per week was never paid.

Alice Pickering was next found living in Leeds, having taken up with a man by the name of Edward Myers. Meanwhile Jane Ellen Smith received a letter from her, in consequence of which Smith came over to Leeds, and was met at the railway station by Pickering. The two spent the day together. On the following day Smith went again to the Lodgings of Pickering, were Alice tried to persuade Smith to take the child back with her to Scarborough. Smith declined. Pickering then said her that mother had written to her to take the child back, and repeated her request for Smith to take the child with her. Still Smith declined. Alice then remarked that she would get money from Myers, the man with whom she was living, and take it herself to Scarborough. She used these words, 'I am going to get into the factory to weave, and I can't get on with him here'. Apparently Pickering had begun to find the obligations of looking after the child too much!

On 25 July there was a railway excursion to Scarborough from Leeds, and on Smith going to the railway station with the intention of returning home, she found Alice Pickering and the child there going to Scarborough on the excursion, and they got into the same carriage. Ellen Smith enquired what Alice was going to do with the child. She replied that she was going to take it to her husband's mother, who would send it to her mother by the carrier on the following day. The train arrived at Scarborough about four o'clock, and the two women separated, but before they parted Smith asked Alice if she was going to take the child at once to her destination. She replied that she was. Subsequently this turned out to be a deceit.

Between four and five o'clock Alice Pickering took her son to the house of a woman called Sarah Turnbull. She was not known to Turnbull, but was acquainted with a person named Massbam, who lived with her. She asked Massbam if she would keep the child and send it on the next day by Coxworth, the carrier, to her mother's house. Massbam refused, and in desperation she then turned to Mrs Turnbull and asked if she would let one of her little girls take the child to her husband's mother, Mrs Allison. Turnbull also refused her entreaties. By this time it was about six o'clock and Alice Pickering and her child left the house, but returned shortly afterwards. There was a little more talk and eventually Turnbull asked Alice what she was going to do with the child. Alice replied that she would take it herself to its grandmother, Mrs Allison. Soon after Alice and the child left in the company of a woman named Sarah Worsnop, but before going she gave the child a sip of beer. The two women and the child walked in a direction almost exactly in contradiction to that in which Mrs Allison's home was situated. They went together as far as a place known as Mr Dove's stonemason's yard, on the outskirts of town and in the direction of an uninhabited part. As they were about to part, the woman Worsnop, who had heard her say that she was going to take the child to its grandmother's, asked Pickering what she was going down there for? She replied that she was going to see a lawyers servant whom she thought would give her something.

It was later learnt that in that direction there is hardly a single house near, and nothing but footpaths, along which people may or may not have been walking between seven and eight o'clock that evening. A little way out there is a stream which roughly speaking, runs at right angles to the road, and passes a small hanging wood about 200 yards in length. The wood is intersected by many paths going zigzag down the bank of the stream. The stream is about four feet wide, and runs rapidly on account of the fall in the ground. The banks of the stream are about two feet high, and are very steep, and such as a child between the age of two and three years would find difficulty in scaling for the purpose of getting out of the stream should it fall in.

Worsnop and Alice parted about 6.40 pm, and the two Alice and child, were next seen by Thomas Harrison, a joiner, who was on a piece of ground known as the Cricket Field, about 400 yards away from the two who were in a field at the top of the hanging wood. Harrison had a spyglass, and he saw them going along a road, and then leave the road and make for a shed. On approaching the shed he observed that the woman saw a man, whereupon she turned and went to a stile which led into the wood. The two, woman and child entered the wood and were lost to Harrison's view.

After that nothing was known what happened to the child by the evidence of eyewitnesses.

Figure 73. *Interior of Scarborough Railway Station.*

Later, that evening at about a quarter to eight o'clock, Alice Pickering turned up at the house of Ellen Jane Smith in an agitated condition. Smith went with Alice to Scarborough Railway Station (Figure 73), it being the latter's intention to return to Leeds. On the way Smith asked her where the child was, and Alice replied that she had left the child at Tom's mother's (meaning her mother-in-law). Smith left her at the railway station talking to a man called Nicholls. She also told Nicholls that she had taken the child to its grandmother's and that she would get paid for it, as she know were Tom Myers, her son, was.

On 5 August a man named Thomas Simpson, who rented some fields in the neighbourhood of the hanging wood previously mentioned, was going home to his dinner about the middle of the day, when at the lower end of the water in the wood he found the body of a child lying face down in the stream. The water there was about eighteen inches deep, and the body had apparently been caught in the middle of the stream. Simpson did not lift the body out, but went and brought two detectives officers named Johnstone and Thompson, who came and took the corpse to the mortuary. There a post mortem examination was made by Dr Taylor, Medical Officer for the Borough. That gentleman was of the opinion that the body must have been in the water at least six or seven days. The child had been well clothed and cared for, and the prosecution thought it exceedingly improbable that it could have been left by the mother to take its chance, and that after rambling about it became weak for want of food and exhaustion and simply dropped into the water. The body was duly identified by the two women Mary Ann Major and Ellen Jane Smith, and Alice Pickering was taken into custody at Leeds by Detective Officer Thompson.

On her way to Scarborough Pickering told that officer that she took the child to that town by a trip, and left it at Mrs Allison's. Afterwards she confessed, 'I did not tell you right...' Later she made a more detailed statement to Superintendent Pattison, after being cautioned. This statement read:

> *I took my child to Mrs Major's, Clarence Place. I was to pay 4s 6d a week for it, but I could not pay it. I got to know Myers in the Militia, and went to Leeds with him. He treated me and the child well until the father got to know and forced him to leave me. I did not know what to do. I was destitute, and wrote to a girl called Smith to come to me at Leeds, and she came. I asked her to take the child to my friends. She refused. I brought it myself and took it myself to a home in Falsgrave (Figure 74), near which my husband's mother lives, and asked them to take it in, as I was afraid to go myself. They refused,*

Figure 74. *Falsgrave, now a suburb of Scarborough.*

*and said they would have nothing to do with either me or my child. I
did not know what to do with it. I could not keep it. I had no money
nor no place where I could take it to, so I took it over the fields and
left it, thinking some person would find it and take care of it, but I
never put it in the water.*

The prosecution submitted that if a mother, whose duty it was to
feed and clothe and take care of a child, left it in such a place and
such a situation that it was probable, in the expectation of the
mother, that harm, possibly resulting in death, might happen to the
child, that would amount to murder. It had been previously held in
another case that a mother, who left her child in an orchard covered
with leaves and where such an unlooked for event as a bird of prey
striking that child could happen, she was guilty of murder. The child
in question was apparently able to take care of itself. It was for the
jury to decide whether, after being left in the wood by the mother, it
would not be likely to seek an exit from the wood, and would not be
capable and also willing to avoid going near the edge of the rapid
stream. If the jury felt a reluctance to come to the conclusion that
human instincts prevented the unfortunate girl from taking such a
terrible course as to put her own child into the water herself, it was
possible for them to find that the child was left under such
circumstances – such, as for instance, she left it sitting on the bank
close to the edge of the water – then it was probable, to the
knowledge of the mother – nay, it was almost a certainty, – that the
child would fall into the stream. I such a case the crime of which the
mother would be guilty, would be murder.

Mr Fenwick, defense counsel, in the course of an able address to
the jury on the prisoner's behalf, contended that the whole of the
evidence showed unmistakably that the intention of the girl was to
abandon the child in the hope, as she has declared, that some one
would find it and care for it. He suggested that the beck was in flood,
and that the child itself may have fallen into the water.

His Lordship cautioned the jury against being led by Mr Fenwick's
offer of a verdict of manslaughter from what might prove their
painful duty of regarding the charge of wilful murder. They must
discharge their duty like men, not like children, not from sympathy
or false delicacy, but according to the evidence. The learned counsel
for the defense had referred to the absence of any marks such as
might be expected if the face of the deceased had been pressed down
against the bottom of the beck; but it would be equally murder if the
prisoner simply pushed the child into the water, so as to cause its

death, or knowing that death would probably result, if she abandoned her child there at eight o'clock on a wet night. Such a desertion was, in the mildest view, not consistent with that natural motherly affection which Mr Fenwick had pleaded as an argument against supposing that the unfortunate girl at the bar could be guilty of the crime with which she was charged.

The jury retired, and after an absence of about half an hour, they returned with a verdict of guilty, the foreman adding, however, that after due consideration of the whole circumstances they unanimously and strongly recommended the prisoner to mercy.

His Lordship assumed the black cap, and passed sentence of death. In doing so, he said:

Alice Pickering, a merciful jury have felt that they had no other course to adopt than to find you guilty of the serious crime with which you are charged, and I have no hesitation in saying that I concur in their verdict. They have also added a strong and unanimous recommendation to mercy. It will be my duty to forward that to our Gracious Majesty the Queen, who is the fountain of all mercy, and with the exercise of whose perogatives I have noting whatever to do. My duty is limited to passing upon you the sentence of the law, and I shall not enlarge upon the facts of the case. That is no part of my duty, but I hope you will moved to sincere penitence with regard to what must have occurred on the night of the 28 July.

The prisoner, Alice Pickering, though evidently realising her awful position, heard her sentence without exhibiting any sign of emotion, and was able, with the slight assistance of a warder, to descend the stairs leading from the dock to the cell and her eventual fate.

Chapter 16

A Poor Little Fisher Lad –
William Papper (1868-82)

n Thursday, 5 January 1882, Osmand Otto Brand, skipper and part owner of the Hull-based fishing smack *Rising Sun* entered the Parliament Street Police Station in the port of Hull and spoke to Police Sergeant William Elliott. Brand told the duty officer that he wished to report the fact that one of his crew had fallen overboard at sea and subsequently drowned. The following is the entry made by Police Sergeant Elliott in the Station Occurrence Book:

> *Osmand Otto Brand, residing at Harrow House, Hessle Road, Hull and skipper and owner of the smack Rising Sun, reports that at about 5.30 am on the 1st of January 1882, they were trawling on the fishing ground about 120 miles from Spurn, when the cook, William Papper, 14 years of age, a native of Hull, was knocked overboard by the big foresail sheet and drowned. The smack was put about, and every effort was made to save him, but without avail. The body was not recovered.*

At that point in time there was little to suggest that Captain Brand was anything but remorseful about the loss of the young fisher-lad and that he was stating anything but the truth. Brand knew the Papper family fairly well and had told the boy's father of the tragedy prior to reporting it to the police.

William Papper had been apprenticed to Osmand Brand by his father Joseph Papper in April 1881. It was to have been a seven-year apprenticeship. William had gone to sea on Thursday, 17 December 1881. This was the last time his father had seen him alive. Apparently he was quite excited about the voyage and was keen to please the captain. Joseph Papper must have been himself quietly pleased to see the *Rising Sun* moored in Albert Dock on Thursday, 5 January 1882. He approached the vessel and was met by Osmand Brand who bid him good-day, then went on to announce the news of Williamís demise.

> *I've very bad news to tell you. Your little boy got knocked overboard by the big foresail on New Year's morning. I was down below, and they came and told me the boy was overboard. I ran up the ladder and let*

go the stopper to bring the ship round, but we could see nothing of him.
He was called up at half past five in the morning, to get the breakfast
ready, and they called him forward to help take the big foresail in.

Accidents at sea were quite a common occurrence around seaports.
The tragic loss was accepted by both the family and authorities alike.
After a brief investigation that involved questioning the other crew
members, one or two ambiguities existed, but nothing remained to
cause too much concern. As far as it was practical, the subject was
closed and would have remained so if it had not been for William
Dench, one of the crew of the *Rising Sun*. William John Dench
walked into a police station and made the following statement which
completely altered the facts of the matter.

I reside at 18 Staniforth Place, Hessle Road, Hull, and am second
hand of the smack Rising Sun owned by Osmand Otto Brand, who
is also captain of the smack. About Thursday, 17th December last, I
left Hull for the fishing ground in the Rising Sun as second hand,
there being on board Mr Brand, the captain; Frederick Rycroft, the
third hand; David Yates, deck chap; William Blackburn, apprentice;
and William Papper, cook and apprentice. After the smack left Albert
Dock she brought up at Sunk Island, and remained there all night.
After we had cast anchor I was on deck with the captain and crew,
when I heard the captain say to Papper 'Get me a lacing' [a lacing
is a short length of rope used to tie the mainsail up]. *Papper went*
down into the cabin, and the captain followed him, as likewise did
Blackburn. I was standing on the deck at the companion ladder,
which leads to the cabin, when I heard the captain say, 'Now you
bugger, I'll pay you for telling lies about me. I have something to do
with your sister haven't I?' The boy commenced to cry, and said, 'I
never said so.' He [the captain] then began to thrash him, and as he
did so, he said, 'Now you bugger, I have had something to do with
your sister, and I'll do you'. I then went down into the cabin and
found the skipper beating Papper with a short piece of rope about one
and a half inches in thickness, with a knot at each end. He thrashed
him for about five minutes. He struck him repeatedly on the head and
face, and I saw the boy's nose bleeding, and his lips were swollen. The
captain then told him to get washed, and called him a mucky bugger.
The boy was crying, and appeared very much hurt from the beating
he had received. Papper then at the captain's request, got the tea.

On Friday, the 23rd December, about nine o'clock in the morning
we were about 90 miles from Spurn Light. I was on the deck helping
to mend the trawling line nets, when I heard the skipper say to Papper,

'Now this is all through you,' referring to the damage the net had sustained through the warp having fouled, and I saw him strike Papper a blow with his clenched fist in the face, which knocked him down. He then ordered him to go forward, and stop there for three days, calling him a bugger at the same time. The lad at once got up. He was crying from the effects of the blow, and went forward. The captain followed him and said to him, 'Get up on that stay', pointing to it. Papper, who was still crying, did not get up, and the captain then said, 'You won't get up? Then I'll make you', and he then went up and got a bucket, which had a rope tied to it, and he dipped the bucket overboard and drew it up full of water, and threw it over him. He repeated this treatment five or six times. The lad then said, 'Don't throw any more water over me and I'll get up'. The captain then said harshly, 'get on there', and I saw the lad mount the stay. He was wet through. The skipper then went to a small boat which was on deck, got a handspike and took it forward, and, handing the handspike to Papper, he said, 'Here take hold of this'. The lad Papper took the handspike, and he did as he was told, holding on by one hand to the stay, and with the other hand he held the handspike with an end resting on the rail. The skipper then told us to go aft and get our dinners and we did so. Whilst we were having our dinners the captain went back on deck, and I followed about ten minutes afterwards. I then saw the skipper in the act of thrashing Papper with a rope end. Papper at that time was on the deck forward, and he had apparently got down from the place were we left him. I heard the captain say to him, 'get up on that stay, you bugger'. Papper was crying, and did not get up, and I saw the skipper strike him several blows in the face with his clenched fist. Papper was lying on the deck, and the skipper was bending over him and striking him with his fist. The captain next took hold of him by the back of his guernsey, and dragged him aft to a spot about six feet from the windlass, and papper then got onto his knees, and was about to go aft when the skipper dealt him several blows with the end of a rope. The skipper then got the lantern halliards and tied them under Papper's arms, and as he did so, he said, 'I'll hang you, you bastard'. The lad cried, 'Oh, don't hang me'. The captain then put the end of the halliards round the winch, and called Blackburn to him. Blackburn then winched and turned the handle, Papper was drawn up about four feet from the deck. The skipper held on to Papper's legs to steady him, whilst being hauled up he screamed loudly, the crosstree holding the lantern halliards broke and Papper fell heavily onto the deck. Papper seemed to be insensible and was sent forward to the stem by the captain.

The next morning (Saturday) about eight o'clock before Christmas, I was on deck, and I saw the captain and Papper forward. At the time I saw the skipper he was beating Papper with a rope end. Papper was standing up on deck, and I saw the skipper leave off rope ending him, and he struck him a heavy blow on the side of the head with his clenched fist, which knocked him down. I saw him jump onto Papper with both feet. He jumped onto his chest, and knelt on him - on the chest, and reached for a rope, which was near and tied it round his neck and pulled both ends tight. It appeared to me that he was endeavouring to strangle him. I then rushed forward and took hold of the captain by the shoulder and said, 'Leave off, or you will be killing the lad'. He said, 'I don't care, I'll kill the bugger'. He then got off Papper and I stopped down and untied the rope from Papper's neck...

His statement continued to detail the most horrendous torture imaginable. Passage after passage outlined the inhumane deeds Brand inflicted on the young lad. Heaven knows what thoughts passed through the mind of William Papper during the final hours of his life. Indeed, death must have come as something of a blessed relief compared to the living hell he suffered on board the *Rising Sun* over that Christmas period.

At six o'clock on New Year's Day, the young lad finally succumbed and died from the terrible beatings and ill-treatment he received on that voyage. The confession of William Dench described his final hours and the ignominious end of William Papper it graphic detail.

...He was dead. His eyes were black, and his countenance disfigured. The captain said, 'What shall we do with him?' I said, 'I don't know he is your apprentice'. He said, 'We shall have to throw him overboard, he is too disfigured, we dare not take him back to Hull. You must keep David [Yates] on deck, and not let him see him, because I cannot trust him. He will spoil all. You are all in it as well as me'. The next morning at three o'clock, the skipper called me out and said, 'Give us a hand to get papper on deck'. I got up and went to the bunk where the corpse was and assisted the captain, Rycroft and Blackburn to carry it on deck again. The skipper then came down, and he got the deceased's clothes – trousers, shirt, and braces – and went on deck again. About half past five Rycroft came to the companion ladder and called out to me and the captain, 'Jump up here, Papper is overboard...

Captain Brand and Frederick Rycroft, the main perpetrators of this wicked crime, were arrested at once. Brand actually claimed that he was innocent of the deed and that each member of the crew were as

Figure 75. *A prison hanging - this type of execution replaced public hangings.*

guilty of the crime, if not more so, than he. The East Riding Constabulary, however, took little notice of his malicious ramblings. The two of them, Brand and Rycroft, were tried for the murder of William Papper at Hull Assizes shortly afterwards (Figure 75). William Dench, prompted by the burden of his guilt, escaped trial by turning Queen's evidence.

Unfortunately, many of the local people did not view actions of Dench in the same way as he intended. A contemporary local newspaper reported.

The details of the alleged murder have created tremendous excitement amongst the fishing community of South Myton, and singularly enough the tide of popular indignation has set against William John Dench, the man whose statements led to the apprehension of Brand, the skipper of the Rising Sun. Dench resides at 18 Staniforth Place, Hessle Road, and yesterday morning his house was beseiged by a large number of persons, who loudly declared their intentions of lynching him. Dench, with difficulty escaped, and the crowd was cleared away by the policeman who was on duty in that neighbourhood. The man was, however, followed by a dozen others, and it would have fared ill with him had he got into their hands. Fortunately for him he managed to keep clear of those who were on watch for him. Doubtless he will receive the protection of the police, as his evidence against Brand, the skipper, is of the gravest character...

Chapter 17

The Case of the Disappearing Corpse! –
George Stephenson (*d.*1884)

During the early months of 1884, a most extraordinary and mysterious affair excited the population of the village of Cayton (Figure 76), near Scarborough, and occupied a considerable staff of the North Riding Constabulary. A girl named Elizabeth Stevenson, not yet out of her teens, had been in the service of Mr Anderson, of Osgodby, which lies to the east of Cayton. Sometime in late November or early December of the previous year she came home to Cayton with her illegitimate child. Her parents were small farmers, and occupied a red brick house fronting the road leading through the village with farm buildings etc in the rear. When the girl came home, arrangements were made for the babe to be confined at the house of an old couple named Atkinson, who lived directly opposite her parents.

Figure 76. *Cayton village, North Yorkshire.*

At the beginning of January 1884, the child being ill, it was seen by Dr William Peck Haworth. The child, however, died on Saturday, 13 January 1884, and Mr Haworth was asked to furnish the usual death certificate, but something unusual excited his suspicions and he declined to do so, and told both the girl and her mother, Ann Stevenson, that an inquest would be necessary. This determination of Mr Haworth raised the anger of both women and they berated him pretty soundly, but he very properly communicated with Police Constable Robson, stationed in the village. The officer then informed Inspector Dove, with the result that Mr Jennings, of Driffield, the coroner, was also contacted, and he directed that a *post mortem* examination of the body should be made on the following Tuesday morning, and an inquest in the afternoon.

The body of the child was in charge of Mr and Mrs Atkinson, and the Stevensons had a coffin made, and the body temporarily placed in it, as the parties were warned not to seal it or interfere with the corpse until the doctor had made his examination. And now comes the mysterious part of the singular affair.

On the Monday night before the day of the *post mortem*, 15 January, shortly before eleven o'clock, it appeared the Stevensons invited the Atkinsons to go to their house and sit with their son, who had to be up on account of a horse being ill. The Atkinsons went, securing their habitation by taking out the thumb piece of the door sneck, so that no one could enter without inserting some similar thin material. They remained at the Stevensons until two o'clock on Tuesday morning, and when they returned to their own house, they found that although the coffin was in place in which the body of the child had been left, the body had vanished!

This fact speedily came to the knowledge of Superintendent Spence and Inspector Dove, and early on Tuesday morning with other officers they instituted a strict search, in which they were soon after joined by Mr James Haworth, MRCS, the surgeon, in practice at Filey, and his son Dr William, the former of whom had come for the express purpose of making the post mortem. Wells, drains, and all sorts of out of the way places were carefully scrutinised without result by Superintendent Spence, Inspector Dove, and Sergeant Heald, the two females meanwhile being watched in the house by PC Robson. After some time was spent in searching outside, the search moved indoors, and Superintendent removed the ashes, etc, from the fire grate, and he had no sooner proceeded to do this than there was a marked change in the demeanour of the two females. A careful examination of the ashes was made, and Dr Haworth took charge of

Figure 77. Star Inn, *Cayton, in the nineteenth century.*

a considerable portion. Whilst this examination was going on outside at the rear of the house, the elder female asked Robson's permission to go upstairs, which was granted, but in a few minutes, hearing an extraordinary noise overhead, he rushed upstairs, followed by the girl Elizabeth Stevenson, and there they found the mother Ann Stevenson had suspended herself by means of a roller towel to a beam in the room, and was well nigh strangled. Robson released her at once, and shortly after both the mother and daughter were charged on suspicion of murdering the child, and were conveyed to the police station at Falsgrave by Inspector Dove, accompanied by Sergeant Heald.

While this was being enacted, the jury, who had been summoned to the inquest at the *Star Inn*, Cayton, began to assemble (Figure 77). Shortly before the appointed hour, three o'clock, Mr Trigg, the deputy coroner, also arrived. As soon as the whole of the jury assembled, Superintendent Spence related the facts connected with the disappearance of the body. In response, the deputy coroner told the jury that under the circumstances he could not swear them in, there being nothing before them over which to hold an inquest, and his only alternative was to discharge them. With regard to the customary fee, he said he could not pay that, as they were not sworn, but he would take their names and lay the question before the proper authority.

At that point, the matter was concluded with the two women being first brought before the bench of the North Riding Magistrates Court at Scarborough on Thursday, 17 January 1884. Here the prosecution told the Magistrates, presided over by Alfred D'Arley, that they had fully intended to go ahead and try the case, but that although time had been given for Dr Scattergood, of Leeds to analyse the remains found in the ashes, they had had a letter from the doctor stating that he could not possibly complete his analysis in the fourteen days allowed. Further, the prosecution added that after careful attention to the evidence at hand there was insufficient to establish the charge of willful murder against the prisoners. The prosecution therefore intended to reduce the charge to one of ordinary indictable misdemeanor; and asked if it were convenient to the bench that the case be adjourned for three weeks, when the prosecution would be prepared to prefer such a charge against the two women as the evidence might allow.

The case was thus about to be remanded at this stage of the hearing, when a difficulty arose concerning bail. As the charge had effectively been withdrawn, technically the two prisoners were not under charge and the question of bail did not arise, they should be dismissed as free. And if there was no charge, then they could also not be indicted at the next Assizes. The prosecution therefore, had to make a charge. In response, the prosecution charged the two with 'preventing the burial of a dead body', which was an indictable misdemeanor – an offence against common law, and that was the charge they should make before the court for the remand. The magistrates, however, felt the charge insufficient and requested that the charge should be clarified further before the prisoners could be indicted at the next Assizes. After some delay, an exact wording was agreed which read; 'That they did unlawfully and wickedly arrest, take and carry away the dead body of George Stevenson, to prevent the internment and burial of the said dead body, at Cayton, in the North Riding of the County of York, on the 15th day of January

1884'. The elder prisoner was further indicted for having attempted to commit suicide by hanging herself. Bail was thus agreed and a date set for the trial.

In due course the Ann Stevenson, aged fifty years, and Elizabeth Stevenson, aged twenty-two appeared before the Yorkshire Assizes at Leeds before Mr Justice Hawkins.

The prosecution in the form of Mr Skidmore lead by stating that the offence was a somewhat novel crime in England, though there had been a recent case of the kind in Wales. The crime with which the prisoners were charged was a common law misdemeanor. He then went on to lay out the facts in some finer detail. The younger prisoner was on 17 December 1883, in the service of Mrs Anderson, at Osgodby, in the North Riding. On the date named she gave birth to a child, which on the nineteenth she took to the house of Mrs Atkinson, whom she knew, and left it in Mrs Atkinson's care for a few weeks. On 9 January the infant, which was in good health, was fetched back to the house of the prisoners, which was opposite to Mrs Atkinson's. The following morning the child became seriously ill. One of the prisoners gave it food, but it grew worse. The following day, 11 January, the doctor was called but it died. The rest has been outlined above.

In their defence, Mr Stuart-Wortley stated that while there is no argument that the corpse disappeared, however, the body was removed by the two accused for the purpose of cremation, and as such, there had been no crime. He contended that the coroner had no authority to order an inquest to be held. He alluded to the Welsh cremation case as bearing out this contention.

His Lordship reminded defence, however, that if it is shown that the prisoner's burnt the body to defeat the coroner's intention to examine the body for the purposes of collaborating a crime, then that will be an offence. The coroner had information which, assuming the circumstances to be true, made an inquest expedient. It does not follow that the information was true, but it was sufficient to give him the right to exercise his discretion and hold an inquest, especially if he consider that the death was not the result of natural causes.

During trial witnesses were called to determine if in fact, the child had died of unnatural causes. None were able to say so. Mr T Scattergood, MRCS, and lecturer on medical jurisprudence to the Leeds School of Medicine, gave the result of his examination of the ashes submitted to him. Some of the charred bones he stated were not human, but others he had no doubt, were the calcined bones of a very young child, in particular he could identify the skull of a newly born infant among the rabbit and hare bones. But other than identify the bones he could not say of what the child died.

In conclusion the prosecution failed to prove that the two women had wilfully murdered the child George Stevenson either by poison in the food or by other means. However, they were found guilty by the jury of the lesser charge of burning the body of a dead child for the purpose of evading an inquest.

At the Yorkshire Assizes, at Leeds, on Monday last (4 August 1884) Ann and Elizabeth Stevenson, mother and daughter respectively, were placed at the bar to receive sentence.

Mr Stuart-Wortley who appeared for Ann Stevenson, addressing his Lordship, said the persons were two ignorant villagers who knew nothing of the law, and had nothing in their mind but the shame of having an illegitimate child and the natural repulsion to a *post mortem* examination. He hoped his Lordship would under the circumstances pass as lenient a sentence as possible.

Mr Mellor, who appeared for Elizabeth Stevenson, pointed out that until recently it was not known that the act of the prisoners constituted an offence at law.

His Lordship said this was the first offence of the kind in the country, but if there was a repetition, severe punishment would follow. He sentenced each to two months' imprisonment without hard labour.

Chapter 18

A Woman Beaten to Death –
Maria Stonehouse (1848-94)

he *Scarborough Evening Gazette* reported on Thursday, 1
November 1894 that,

*A shocking tragedy occurred at Filey on Saturday night,
when a long series of quarrels between husband and wife culminated
in the death of the latter, and the arrest of her husband on a charge
of murder. Such an event is believed to be without parallel in the
history of this quiet little watering-place, and the fact that the ill-
matched couple are so well-known in the town makes the affair, in the
eyes of the inhabitants, all the more shocking.*

The woman in question, beaten to death, was Maria Stonehouse,
almost 46 years old. She and her husband, Samuel Stonehouse,
together with their two children, Samuel Dixon aged 14 and Sarah
about 12 years, had lived for upwards of ten years in a house in
Barnett's-yard, Queen Street, Filey, and it was in the kitchen of that
house that the tragedy took place (Figure 78). There were no
witnesses to the occurrence, but there is no doubt that the affair

Figure 78. *Queen Street, Filey, in the nineteenth century.*

commenced as only a repetition of many similar brawls. The husband, having drawn his wages, appears to have gone to a public house, the *Star Inn*. His wife followed with the intention of getting some money for the rent before it was drunk away, and both of them returned to their home. Words fell to blows, and soon after six o'clock on 27 October, the wife ran out of the house and took refuge with a neighbour named Martha Gedge. Her husband followed her, and after another attack on her person, she returned home by a different route having first called in at a relative's called Birr. Returning himself to their house, the husband found his wife there with their daughter Sarah and appears to have attacked her with great ferocity and he finally struck the wife a tremendous blow behind the ear with a firebrick, supposedly fracturing her skull. The son at this point came home from work and discovered the scene and the little boy ran into the street accompanied by his sister, and informed a grown-up son of Mrs Stonehouse, William Wood Proctor of what was taking place. He immediately went for the police, and returned in a few minutes with Sergeant Clarkson, from nearby John Street, who is stationed in the town and another man Amos Danby. Upon entering the house they found Maria Stonehouse lying on the sofa moaning, and with blood flowing from a wound at the back of her head. Her husband was sitting in a chair in front of the fireplace in the same room in his stocking feet. A quantity of crockery and meat was strewn about the floor. It was at once evident that the woman was seriously injured, and Mr Hugh Orr, surgeon, who lives close at hand, was called in. Nothing he could do, however, proved of any avail, and Mrs Stonehouse succumbed to her injuries about half past seven o'clock. Her husband, Samuel Stonehouse was at once taken into custody and removed to the police station at Filey.

An initial examination of the body showed it to be covered with bruises, whilst the deceased's left arm was broken. This was no doubt due to her attempting to save herself when struck down by the husband.

Both husband and wife appear to have been intemperate, and their drunken quarrels in the past were the talk of the town, and the tragedy ending their married life did not come as great a surprise to the many who knew them both. Indeed, only a short time before the final tragedy, Stonehouse had left his wife after one of their periodical rows, in the course of which she was roughly used, but she had him arrested and sent to prison for six months. Since his return, relations between them it was reported, had been more strained than ever. The neighbours therefore, having grown accustomed to hearing their

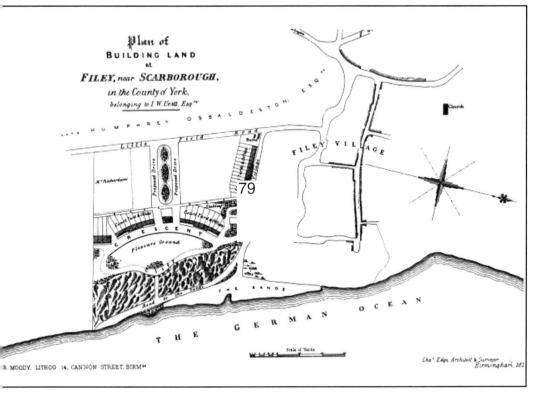

79

Figure 79. *Detail from John W Unett's plan of Filey, 1835, showing the Crescent and adjoining streets.*

arguments and wrangles next door, paid little heed to the proceedings on the Saturday in question, and this undoubtedly accounted for the fact that no one went to the aid of the poor unfortunate spouse.

Samuel Stonehouse, about 50 years of age, was a native of Filey. His wife was Maria Proctor, of Muston, and up to some ten years before they moved to the town, they kept a farm in that village. Since they lived at Filey, the husband earned his livelihood as a bricklayer's labourer. He was described as being a quiet, hard-working man so long as he did not drink, but it was said that he had a dreadful temper on him when roused. The deceased's mother lived in the Crescent, Filey, and her brother Mr Edmund Proctor, took charge of the children (Figure 79).

Stonehouse was first brought before Mr Edwin Martin, JP, at the Filey Court-house on the Monday, and formally charged with having wilfully murdered his wife, Maria Stonehouse, on Saturday 27 October. Police Sergeant R Clarkson was called and gave evidence, which was brief, after which the charge having been read over, the prisoner replied firmly - 'I am not guilty, sir'.

Mr Martin remanded Stonehouse to take his trial at the Bridlington Court on the following week. The prisoner was subsequently remanded to the Hull Goal, where he was to remain until the prescribed day. It is said Stonehouse was not greatly concerned at his fate. The proceedings were attended by Mr Stonehouse, farmer, of Flamborough, and Mr Abraham Stonehouse, of Filey, brothers of the accused.

On Tuesday, the next day, a coroner's inquest was held, following a *post mortem* carried out by Mr Orr assisted by a Dr Stephenson, of Hunmanby. They found thirteen bruises on different parts of the face that appeared to have been caused by a hand or blunt instrument. Upon cutting off the hair they found two wounds on the head, one of which was lacerated. It was believed that the lacerated wound had been caused by the corner of some instrument, and the other by a blunt weapon. The left forearm was bruised and fractured about three inches above the wrist, and the arms, legs and body, front and back, were extensively bruised and battered. In total thirty-nine cuts and bruises were found. All the bruising appeared recent. Upon removing the scalp they found that there was no fracture of the skull. An internal examination found the heart was enlarged, and some of the other organs were diseased. It was given that the immediate cause of death was shock from the injuries received.

The date of Stonehouses's trial was set for Friday, 9 November. Mr Charles Haigh and Mr E R Turton were the counsel for prosecution, and Mr Charles Mellor, defended the prisoner, who pleaded not guilty. Little new evidence was brought before the jury that has not been repeated above.

Mr Haigh, in opening the case, said Stonehouse, his wife and two children were on the day in question living in a cottage in Barnett's-yard, off Queen Street, Filey. The premises originally constituted one dwelling, but had been divided into two cottages, the additional cottage being occupied by a man named William Scott and his family. The division had been effected by the simple process of nailing up a door that separated two of the rooms. This fact was of importance later, because William Scott would state in court that while in his own sitting-room he heard a quarrel and blows in the adjoining room of the prisoner's house.

In closing the case for the prosecution, Mr Haigh submitted that nothing had been elicited to justify the jury in reducing the charge from murder to manslaughter. Although he did not wish to lay too much stress on the threats of Stonehouse in the presence of Mrs Gedge, he thought the jury could not, looking at the later results, lose sight of them.

In his address for the defence, Mr Mellor said the tragedy had its beginnings and ending in drink. Very properly drink had been held to be no excuse for crime, but juries had been advised to consider it when considering with what intent a thing was done. He suggested that when the unfortunate row commenced between the prisoner and his wife there was 'give and take'. The deceased, Maria Stonehouse, had an ungovernable temper, and when in temper she used language that did not make a home very comfortable. Taking everything into consideration, even from the point of view of manslaughter, there was much to be said in favour of the accused. He earnestly pleaded with the jury for a verdict of manslaughter only.

The judge, in summing up, observed that if the jury credited the medical evidence, the woman's death, if not caused, was certainly hastened by the acts of the prisoner. If his acts did not cause, hasten, or contribute to her death, most undoubtedly he was guilty of the offence of manslaughter. He (the judge) could find no possible reason that would justify the jury in acquitting the prisoner altogether. The serious question for them was what was the quality of the prisoner's acts. Did it amount to wilful murder or only to the crime of manslaughter?

The jury after an absence of fifteen minutes, returned into court with a verdict of 'manslaughter'.

The judge, addressing Samuel Stonehouse, said the jury had taken a merciful view of his case, and he had incurred the guilt of manslaughter under circumstances which were extremely serious, he must therefore pass a sentence of equal severity; the prisoner must go to penal servitude for fourteen years.

Chapter 19

Death on the Beach –
Kate Lee (1887-1908)

t nine o'clock one Sunday morning in September 1908, in response to a knock on Withernsea Police Station door, Superintendent Maw opened it to find an excited crowd on the Police Station steps. He was even more taken aback when the nearest man declared in a calm voice, 'I want you to take me in charge'. On asking why, before the man could answer, a voice from the crowd called, 'Oh he has killed a woman on the sands – it's alright, there is a dead body. That's why he wants to be taken in charge!'

Concealing his surprise, the Police Superintendent quickly established that the man wanting to turn himself in was Charles Henry Woodman, twenty-two years of age, and from Hull. To be on the safe side, Maw locked the man in the police cell and then accompanied by the crowd, he made his way to the beach (Figure 80). At the beach, a small boy handed the Superintendent a blood-stained knife and pointed to the body of a teenage girl lying on the

Figure 80. *Withernsea, South Sands.*

Figure 81. *Queen's Hotel, Withernsea, erected in 1903 at a cost of £7,000.*

sand. All around, the crime scene was trampled under the feet of the jostling crowd, and in vain Maw tried to prevent any further destruction of the evidence. His efforts were useless, however, as crowds of locals and day-trippers scrambled everywhere. One morbid individual in particular was found to be collecting the bloodied sand in a child's bucket for a souvenir!

Arranging for the police photographer to take pictures of the scene as best he could and then arranging for the removal of the body, Superintendent Maw then returned to the police station to question Woodman. By this time Woodman had become withdrawn and refused to co-operate would not answer questions about the incident. The Superintendent could not even discover from Woodman the name of the young girl. Eventually, Maw, still unsure of the motive or sequence of events, charged the prisoner with the murder of an unknown woman. He then allowed Charles to wash the blood from his hands.

Figure 82. *The Gardens, Withernsea.*

Notwithstanding Woodman's silence, enquiries soon revealed the deceased to be Kate Lee, a twenty-one year old girl whose home was 41 Edgar Street, Hull, who had been working as a barmaid at the *Queen's Hotel* in the town (Figure 81). Charles Henry Woodman himself, turned out to be a popular member of the staff at the Liverpool Street tramway sheds in Hull who had become infatuated with Miss Lee and had visited her at Withernsea on the Friday prior him giving himself up to the authorities on the Sunday (Figure 82). He had stayed the weekend at Withernsea and had become consumed with jealousy when he saw the girl in company with another man. Woodman had taken Lee to the beach and there he had cut her throat sometime on the Saturday night, returning to the scene next morning where he attracted a large crowd.

In November 1908 Charles Henry Woodman appeared at York Assizes charged with the murder of Miss Kate Lee. During the proceedings it was revealed that his father had spent twenty years in a lunatic asylum and this had some bearing on the prisoner's behaviour. Woodman himself escaped the death sentence by being declared unfit to plead and was ordered by the judge to be detained indefinitely in a secure place.

Chapter 20

A Question of Concealment –
The Suspicious Death of an Illegitimate Child (1909)

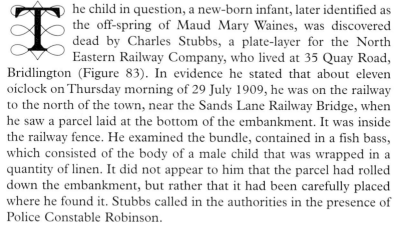

The child in question, a new-born infant, later identified as the off-spring of Maud Mary Waines, was discovered dead by Charles Stubbs, a plate-layer for the North Eastern Railway Company, who lived at 35 Quay Road, Bridlington (Figure 83). In evidence he stated that about eleven oíclock on Thursday morning of 29 July 1909, he was on the railway to the north of the town, near the Sands Lane Railway Bridge, when he saw a parcel laid at the bottom of the embankment. It was inside the railway fence. He examined the bundle, contained in a fish bass, which consisted of the body of a male child that was wrapped in a quantity of linen. It did not appear to him that the parcel had rolled down the embankment, but rather that it had been carefully placed where he found it. Stubbs called in the authorities in the presence of Police Constable Robinson.

Figure 83. *Quay Road, Bridlington.*

A medical gentleman, Dr Forrest made an examination of the corpse at about two oíclock on that same afternoon at the police station. Subsequently he made a *post mortem* examination at the mortuary. His findings were that it was the body of a new-born male child, which, in his opinion, had had a separate existence. It had probably been dead about four days. He did not think it had received any attention at birth. There was an extensive contusion of the scalp, which he thought, was caused before death. The contusion was such that it might have been accompanied by concussion. Except for the contusion, the child appeared quite healthy.

Initially the authorities appeared at a loss in what direction to proceed, and the break-through as to the identity of the mother, was made with the aid of the linen in which the child was wrapped. The sheeting was found to have laundry marks used by a Bridlington Laundry, and once these had been identified, Police Inspector Robson, who had taken charge of the search, was able to place his finger on the person he wanted. The linen on examination consisted of two single bed sheets, one towel, floor cloth, an under-skirt, and an apron. All were very much stained with blood. After the items had been washed, however, Robson discovered on one of the sheets a mark on the inside hem, 'B450', and at another corner, 'AS' and a '4' underneath the letters. The other sheet was marked 'B450' and the towel was likewise marked 'B450', but somewhat indistinctly. The under-skirt was marked 'MW4', and the apron with a black dot and figure four.

As a result of enquiries the whole of the linen articles were traced to 2 Marlborough Terrace, the home of Mrs Edith Crannis. She was able to furnish the identity of the mother. On Saturday, 31 July, Police Inspector Robson called at the house William Botterill, 48 St John Street, Bridlington, where he arrested Maud Mary Waines in the presence of Mrs Louisa Botterill, his wife. He later took away, a number of possessions belonging to the accused including two small bottles of 'Apioline' and some matching aprons bearing the same marks as the one found in he fish bass.

Maud Waines appeared before the East Riding Coroner, Sir Luke White, MP. At the hearing the young girl, whose aged was given as twenty-two, was said to have had the appearance of a girl of 18 or 19 years. She was described as frail and slender. The pallor of her thin, child-like face was death-like, and it was made to appear even greater by the mass of light, straw-coloured hair that covered her head. Even at such a trying time her hair was prettily arranged in coils which extended from the nape of her neck to the top of her head, 'the effect being worthy of a tonsorial artist'.

Naturally she was in a very delicate state of health, and the excitement of her arrest caused her to swoon away on appearing at the proceedings. Her condition was such that Dr Forrest had to be hastily fetched, and under his care she recovered so far as to be able to walk with the assistance of two constables, from the cells to the Court, where she was allowed to sit on a chair at the solicitor's table.

The proceedings before the magistrates were very brief. The Chairman read out the charge which was that on 22 July, in the Borough of Bridlington, she did feloniously, wilfully, and of malice aforethought, kill and murder a certain male child, the child of a certain Maud Waines. The circumstances of the discovery of the body and the inquest were recounted. Maud Waines pleaded not guilty to the charge, and because of her condition, it was decided to adjourn the trial until a later date. Meanwhile, the girl was remanded for a week to Hull prison, where she was to receive proper medical care.

Maud Waines was then assisted from the court, and before the magistrates had finished business, she had commenced her journey to Hull, travelling in company with Inspector and Mrs Robson.

A week later, proceedings recommenced. The prisoner, dressed a in becoming black dress and black hat, was allowed a seat in the well of the court. She looked pale and, it seemed, paler than when she first appeared before the court a week before. Her father, her stepmother, two sisters, and two cousins were seated in the court. The prisoner scarcely raised her eyes from entering the court until leaving it, but on catching sight of her people she was evidently moved.

Mr Wray, for Maud Waines, said on Monday last he had received information that the girl had had an unfortunate relapse – that she was not anything like so well as she had been. He had immediately communicated with Superintendent East and Mr Proctor, deputy County Clerk, who had been instructed to prosecute, and it had been agreed subject to a decision of the bench, to ask for a further adjournment until Tuesday next.

The Chairman said it would have been more regular if a report had been received from the prison doctor, with reference to the prisoner's health.

Mr Wray agreed, but he might add he had himself been to the prison, and he found there was an agreement on the part of those responsible that it would be better that there should be an adjournment for a few days.

As it was anticipated that a hearing of the case would last six or seven hours, the Chairman said the bench were prepared to grant a remand to suit the prisoner. After consultation, the following Tuesday was agreed upon.

Proceedings duly recommenced on the morning of Tuesday 24 August. The *Bridlington Gazette* reported later that the magistrates listened 'to the most sensational story ever told in a local court' and went on to say, 'There are many details which are not fit for publication, and it is only necessary to refer to the Chairman's suggestion that all respectable women, and respectable men, too, should go out of court, to indicate the nature of the case. The women did leave the court - only to group themselves in the lobby, and continue listening to the evidence through the open doorway'.[30]

The prisoner was very much better in health than at any previous time since her arrest. She was quite composed and took an intelligent interest in the witnesses and their evidence. She frequently engaged in conversation with her solicitor, Mr Harry Wray, of the firm Laverack, Son, and Wray, of Hull.

After reading the particulars regarding the finding of the body and subsequent discoveries, Mr Proctor, prosecuting gave a strong hint as to the parentage of the child. He said that in October 1908 Waines was in service at Molescroft, near Beverley, and it was a most extraordinary part of the discoveries made that while there she got into telephonic communication with two men in Hull, and without knowing anything about them, she made an appointment over the telephone to meet them in Beverley.

As a result of the appointment a young man from Hull named Arnold Fisher visited Beverley on 11 November 1908 and in December of that year. Mr Proctor then stressed it was very material that the Justices should bear in mind the dates he had named and also the date when it was suggested that the accused was delivered of a child. This evidence was very material when taken in conjunction with an admission made by Maud Waines on 7 August when she was being taken to Hull prison.

Inspector Robson then told how on 7 August he was conveying the prisoner to Hull prison in a cab from Paragon Station. The cab was stopped on Monument Bridge, Hull (Figure 84), owing to the traffic coming to a halt to allow a procession of a mounted Lancer's regiment to pass. Waines was looking out of the right hand side of the cab, and just as the last section of the regiment had passed, she pointed to a man who was walking by and exclaimed, 'That's the man in a brown suit and straw hat'. He said, 'What man?' She

Figure 84. *Monument Bridge, Hull c.1920.*

replied, 'The baby's father; the baby was just like him. He has a peculiar nose and the baby's nose was just like his. They call him Arnold Fisher and he works at the British Oil Mill Company, Cleveland Street, Hull'. She was very agitated and continued, 'When I told him the state I was in, he said he was going away and would write tome, but I have never seen or heard from him since. No one knows what I have gone through. When I took the baby there, I could hardly leave it. After I had left it, I had to go and have another look at it. I don't think anyone saw me'.

Louisa Botterill, of 48 St John's Street, said she had known the girl Maud Waines since November 1906, when she was in service at Sewerby Vicarage, and was keeping company with her son, Harry Botterill. She approved of the courtship. In May 1907, Mrs Botterill took charge of Waines' illegitimate child and about six weeks after the birth of the child she took up a situation in Bridlington, remaining there until the first week in September. On 26 September 1908 Waines took up a situation at Molescroft, Beverley, leaving again on 1 March 1908. She went to her sister's for a fortnight and then came to stay with her for ten weeks. She then went into the employment of Mrs Crannis, at 2 Marlborough Terrace. She left on 23 July and came to her in a cab about nine o'clock in the morning, bringing with her two tin boxes, a cardboard box, and two hats in brown paper. There was no sign of a new-born infant according to Mrs Botterill. For taking care of Maud Waines' child she received 2s 6d a week from her. She stated that Maud was particularly fond of children and was an affectionate and tender-hearted girl.

Other witnesses were called including Dr A Forrest, Medical Officer of Health for the Borough, who under cross-examination, agreed that 'a fall at birth might have caused the injuries found' on the infant; Morris Sonnefield, a pawnbroker, of Queen Street, Bridlington; Ernest William Hodge, clerk, in the employment of the British Oil Cake Company, Hull and Arnold Fisher, the two men she had telephoned for a 'blind date'; and Harry Campleman, Mrs Botterill's nephew, and an accountant for a company in which Maud Waines had been employed who she contacted about some overdue wages owed to her and whom she had asked to procure some 'Apioline' pills no doubt with a view to trying to terminate her pregnancy.

Lastly, Mrs Edith Crannis, of 2 Marlborough Terrace, Bridlington (Figure 85), gave evidence that the prisoner was in her employment from 19 May to 23 July 1909, and that some days previous to her departure Waines had complained of a pain in her side. She thought it was due to carrying heavy trays upstairs. Mrs Crannis advised her to go to the doctor, Dr McNeill and allowed her time off for that purpose. On 21 July Mrs Crannis gave Waines a week's notice to

Figure 85. *2 Marlborough Terrace, Bridlington, note the cafe.*

leave on account of her weak condition, and also advised her to go back to the doctor again. Waines said she had done so and he had told her she was much better, and would be all right in a few days. Later, she admitted she had not been to a doctor at all. Mrs Crannis was not satisfied and told her she would have to leave immediately, and on a certain accusation being made against her, she replied, 'On no, Mrs Crannis. I wouldn't have come to you in that condition'.

Miss Florence Eden, aged eighteen, who had been in Mrs Crannis' employ since 17 July, corroborated. The case for the prosecution was then concluded, after which, in accordance with the provisions of the *Summary Jurisdiction Act,* the Magistrates' Clerk read over the entire depositions. He had not proceeded for more than five minutes when Maud Waines fainted away in her chair. She recovered in a minute or two, and was removed from the court to return after a delay of five minutes. The reading of the depositions took exactly thirty-five minutes.

Mr Wray in her defence submitted that although there might be some offence of some sort, it could not possibly be so grave a charge as that preferred, and he pointed out how hopeless it was for a jury to convict her on the capital charge in the face of the doctor's evidence. But he wished to say that if they were of opinion that a jury could not convict on the capital charge, they could meet the case by committing her for trail on a much less serious charge.

The Bench retired for consideration and on returning, the Chairman, Mr G Y Lloyd Greame said they had decided that she should be tried at the next Assizes for the murder of her infant child.

Mr Wray did not ask for bail on the grounds of the gravity of the charge and also that the girl felt she was better where she was. He had, however, to apply for legal aid for the prisoner, who had no means whatever. This the Bench promptly granted, and asked Mr Wray to conduct her defence.

The last stage of this painful case was reached at York Assizes on Wednesday, 17 November, when Maud Mary Waines appeared in the dock to answer the charge of concealment of birth, to which she pleaded guilty. This new charge arose from the previous days proceedings, when Mr Justice Bucknill spoke to the Grand Jury and suggested that he did not think any jury in the world would waste their time in finding a true bill for wilful murder. There was a great deal of evidence for a strong case against this unfortunate for having hidden the dead body of her child recently born. He did not wish to say more. This was a terrible case to read. After consideration, the Grand Jury agreed with his Lordship's recommendation and reduced the charge to the one mentioned.

The prisoner was very pale and appeared to feel her position acutely when she appeared in the dock.

Mr Chapman who appeared for Waines, said it was a very sad case, as the prisoner was only a very young woman. She had been in service as a domestic servant, and, unfortunately had fallen, and the result was she had a baby. The baby was born when she was lying unconscious in the bedroom, and she found the child dead on the tiled floor. She had suffered a great deal of pain and grief at the loss of her child.

It was because she did not like to part with the infant that she kept it for a week. Ultimately she decided that she must conceal it. Maud Waines had been in gaol for four months and he would appeal most strongly to his lordship to take the matter into consideration and bind her over. Her father, as a respected and highly thought of working man in Burton Agnes, assured him that he was quite prepared to take her back and give her a good home. Mr Chapman also said he understood some friends of the father, in particular, the Reverend C Hutton-Coates, rector of Burton Agnes, who was familiar with the family, and who had known the girl almost all her life, had interested themselves in the case, and they were endeavouring to get a suitable place for her.

The judge in his address to the Grand Jury asked the girl to listen to him attentively. It was a difficult matter for him to speak about.

The judge proceeded to say that the girl was not alone to blame when in company with that Hull man she identified on the Whitefriargate Bridge. His lordship could not help but feel angry about that man. He ought to have known better then to get the girl into this terrible trouble. He quite understood what the girl did, and he was satisfied the contusion found on the babe's head was caused by a fall onto the tiled floor at a time when she had no one to look after her. It was not done by her. He hoped she would have learnt a lesson, and now turn her back upon the man who had got her into this terrible trouble.

Mr Justice Bucknill then discharged Maud Mary Waines, binding her over in the sum of five pounds to be of good behaviour – and so ended one of the most sensational court cases that Bridlington had ever witnessed; finishing not with an execution, but a triumph of commonsense and justice over prejudice.

Chapter 21

A Clergyman's Suicide –
The Reverend William Lloyd (1866-1909)

On Thursday, 12 August 1909, the Reverend William Stowe Lloyd, aged forty-three, walked under an oncoming train at the Willerby Railway Crossing on Hertford Lane, Willerby, on the section of railway between Seamer and Ganton. The manner of his death caused immense shock in the parish environs.

The Reverend Lloyd had been vicar of Willerby for eighteen months. His parish lay near Kirk Ella in the East Riding, and the cleric had succeeded his father-in-law, the late Reverend George Day who had been vicar between the years 1874 and 1907. The Reverend Lloyd also served as senior curate of St Mary's church, in Scarborough (Figure 86). He was known for his outspoken views and in these he had upset the Church hierarchy on a number of occasions, but he was also noted for his kindness to the elderly and in many quarters his death was a matter of great regret.

There was no parish accommodation at Willerby for the vicar and the Reverend Lloyd lived in North Marine Road, Scarborough with his wife and five children (Figure 87). Occasionally, however, when parish duties necessitated, he stayed with his mother-in-law in the village at the vicarage or at the *Hare and Hounds Inn*.

During his time at Willerby, Lloyd had encountered numerous parochial difficulties, possibly not helped by the fact that the Reverend enjoyed a drink to the extent he had an alcoholic problem. For instance, on 22 June the Vicar's Warden, John Flinton resigned, undoubtedly due to some disagreement between them as on hearing of the death of the Reverend Lloyd, he requested reinstatement to the post! Again, on the Tuesday before his tragic demise, the Archbishop's Clerk had visited the village to collect a petition containing nineteen signatures requesting the removal of the cleric because of his alcoholism. In short, the Reverend William Stowe Lloyd was coming to a crossroads in his life and ecclesiastical career.

Following the tragedy, an inquest was held in Scarborough. The Reverend George Ernest Day, Rector of Aberfoyle, in Scotland, son of the late Rev George Day and brother-in-law of the deceased was

Figure 86. *St Mary's Church, Scarborough.*

Figure 87. *North Marine Road, Scarborough.*

questioned, and the Coroner soon established that action was to be taken by the Ecclesiastical Court to deprive the deceased of his living for numerous serious infringements, possibly even irregularities over Church money. William Dobson, People's Warden at St Luke's church, told how he had been with the deceased that day, checking accounts which had balanced.

Mrs Sophia Day, the Rector's wife, said that she had conversed with the Reverend Lloyd in the vicarage garden on the fateful day, and remarked that the deceased's speech was slurred and his legs were unsteady when he left for Sunday School at a quarter past four o'clock. She added that she did not know of any history of giddiness with the deceased.

The train driver, Frederick Taylor, aged thirty-five, of Garton Terrace, Leeds, had left York at 5.05 pm. When the train was about forty or fifty yards from the Willerby Crossing which would be about 6.30 pm, Mr Taylor saw a man approaching from the right of the track, he blew the whistle as the man appeared oblivious to the danger. At a few yards distance he saw the man look towards the train and step into its path. The driver brought the train to a

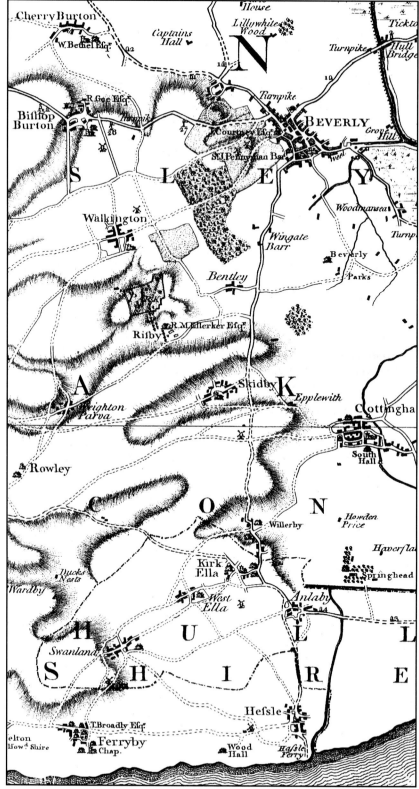

Figure 88. *A detail of Thomas Jeffery's map of Yorkshire dated 1772, showing the village of Willerby just north of Kirk Ella.*

standstill. The Coroner enquired if the deceased had time to cross the track, Taylor replied that he believed so.

Commenting on the Willerby Crossing, the Coroner was informed that the people from Staxton or Willerby intending to catch a train at Ganton Station, use the public footpath from Manor Farm to Low Binnington, then walk alongside he railway track.

A juryman, Mr E Miller, thought an accident was a possibility if the cleric's legs were unsteady. The Coroner stated, 'if in doubt a verdict from the jury of accidental death was not acceptable'. John Flinton, jury foreman, said the majority thought the Reverend Lloyd was temporarily insane and wanted a verdict to this effect. This too was rejected by the Coroner, who stated that all twelve jurymen must be in agreement. Eventually a verdict of suicide while temporarily insane was returned.

A report in the *Scarborough Mercury* on the burial service stated:

At Willerby on Saturday afternoon, the funeral of the late W.S. Lloyd took place amidst every manifestation of regret. The Reverend A.C. Blunt, Vicar of Ganton and the Vicar of Scarborough (Archdeacon Lindsay), officiated. Large numbers of clerical and lay friends of the deceased were present.

The account for the funeral was paid on the 30 October 1909, and amounted to £5 7s 0d. Eight bearers carried the deceased from the vicarage to the church, their names and fees: Thomas Flinton, 2s 6d; William Binks, 2s 6d; John Ireland, 2s 6d; George Nesfield, 2s 6d; William Cooper, 2s 0d; Hornsby Sedman, 2s 0d; William Brown, 2s 0d; Henry Chew, 2s 0d; Fred Dobson, sexton, 3s 0d.

Throughout the burial service the coffin remained in the porch, unable to be brought into the Church, as the occupant was a suicide. The Reverend William Stowe Lloyd was buried in an unmarked grave near the boundary hedge opposite the east window of Willerby Church (Figure 88).

Chapter 22

A Case of
Carbolic Acid Poisoning –
Mrs Mary Lazenby (*d.*1909)

ir Luke White, MP, County Coroner, on the afternoon of Tuesday, 17 August 1909, held an inquest on the body of Mrs Mary Lazenby, wife of Mr W Lazenby, retired Chief Railway Traffic Inspector, whose death occurred the same morning under sad and tragic circumstances.

The bereaved husband stated that his wife was 65 years of age. She had been depressed during the passed few weeks, and had been attended by Dr Wetwan, Medical Officer for the Bridlington District. That morning (17 August), about a quarter to seven o'clock, Mrs Lazenby had gone out of the bedroom with a glass in her hand. She had gone, he thought, for a drink of cold water, fresh drawn, which the doctor had recommended she take regularly. She returned within two or three minutes whereupon she threw open the bedroom door, and looking at her husband in bed, cried, 'I have poisoned myself'. He asked, 'Whatever with?' and she replied, 'Carbolic'. The wife then went round to her side of the bed and began to stagger. The husband immediately went to her aid, and lifted her onto the bed. He tried to get her to speak, but could not, so he at once summoned the daughter, going to her bedroom, while a servant was dispatched immediately for Dr Wetwan.

Meanwhile, Mr Lazenby's daughter, Mrs Lucy Tinegate, came into the bedroom and suggested an emetic. Mustard and water were applied, but to no purpose. Dr Wetwan came shortly afterwards.

When questioned, the husband thought the wife died about seven o'clock - not more than fifteen minutes after she first left the room. She had never previously threatened to do any violence to herself, and he had no reason to suppose she would have done so. The carbolic he stated was kept in the bathroom in a bottle. It was kept there for sanitary purposes, and he had no idea there was any in the house at the time. The bottle was found on a shelf under the basin in the bathroom. Mrs Lazenby had put the bottle back again, after corking it. The glass was on the little table near, adjoining the wash basin. The glass was empty, and there was a slight sediment in it. Mr

Lazenby had no idea how much carbolic was in the bottle when she took it.

Mrs Lucy Florence Tinegate, the daughter, gave evidence that she had seen her mother the previous evening, and she seemed rather more depressed if anything. She had next seen her mother that morning lying across the bed, but she appeared quite unconscious then. She did not speak. Mrs Tinegate did not know the carbolic was in the bathroom, though she knew it was used in the house for sanitary purposes. It was on a shelf when she found it, along with other bottles. She did not know the cause for her depression. Mrs Lazenby had been bad in the last attack, about five weeks previous.

Dr Wetwan said he had been attending the deceased for about six weeks. She had been suffering from nervous debility, accompanied by great mental depression but he could not state for what reason she was so depressed. Mrs Lazenby had been a good deal better the last time he had seen her – three or four days before. He last saw the deceased about seven o'clock that morning. She was on the bed, and had apparently only just died. He made an external examination. The appearance of the body pointed to carbolic poisoning; evidently crude carbolic acid had been used.

The jury returned a verdict of death from carbolic acid poisoning, while the deceased was of unsound mind.[31]

Chapter 23

The Bishop Burton Tragedy –
The Death of Edward Dunn (*d.*1909)

r Justice Bucknill opened the autumn Assizes for the city of York at the Guildhall on the morning of Tuesday 16 November 1909. The procession from the Mansion House to the Guildhall consisted of the following the order given; the Chief Constable (Mr J Burrow); the Under Sheriff (Mr J Peters); the Town Clerk (Mr H Craven); the Reverend Dr Solloway (Lord Mayor's Chaplain); the sword and mace bearers; Mr Justice Bucknill; the Lord Mayor (Alderman J Birch); the City Sheriff (Councillor W A Forster-Todd); and Alderman Agar and Alderman Border (City Magistrates).

His Lordship, Mr Justice Bucknill, in his address to the Grand Jury, said they would have already seen the calendar, and he regretted to tell them that they had not a light one to deal with. There were no less than three charges of murder, and he proposed to speak about them all.

The first case was that of Harry Gilbank for the willful murder of Edward Dunn at Bishop Burton on 19 September instant (Figure 89). 'This is a very extraordinary case', remarked his lordship, 'and one which has taken me some time to master in its details, and one which will give you [the jury] some trouble. There has been an extraordinary complication of circumstances here'.

James Fee, a labourer, is charged with the manslaughter on a coroner's inquisition, of Edward Dunn, and the other man, Harry Gilbank, is charged with the willful murder of the same man. There is no doubt that this case arose out of the drunken condition of affairs that existed on 19 September when some harvesters, apparently Irishmen, were in a certain public house with others in Bishop Burton, and they and others were turned out of the public house or went out on the high road, and on the high road, not far from the public house, the poor unfortunate body of Dunn was found the same night.

The dates, however, were somewhat odd, and the judge directed the Grand Jury's attention to them. The 19 September was the date of the alleged murder. On 20 September James Murray, James Fee,

Figure 89. *Bishop Burton, East Yorkshire.*

and Arthur Ashworth were taken before Mr Hudson, a magistrate at Beverley, charged with the murder of Edward Dunn. The following day, when in custody, Fee elected to give evidence before a coroner's jury and so did James Murray and Arthur Ashworth. The result of that decision was that James Fee now stood committed on the Coroner's Inquisition, for the manslaughter of Dunn. The next date of significance was 25 September, when Murray, Fee and Ashworth came again before the justices still charged with willful murder, and the magistrates remanded the case until the 30 September.

Meantime, on 27 September, Harry Gilbank, who was now charged with willful murder, and a man named Thorne, were charged before the justices with murder, and evidence was given of their arrest on 26 September at Beverley on certain statements made by Thorne to the police. On 30 September the prosecution was withdrawn against Murray, Fee and Ashworth, although the charge of manslaughter was still held against Fee arising out of the Coroner's Inquisition. The case was further adjourned until 7 October. On that date, further evidence was adduced and Fee, who was by this date free on police bail, gave evidence; but not a word did he say against Gilbank. He did not see Gilbank do anything and he did not hear him do anything. James Murray also gave evidence and so did Ashworth. The justices having heard the evidence, discharged the man Thorne, leaving Harry Gilbank, however, to face a charge of willful murder.

'A more extraordinary case, during the eleven years I have been on the bench, and the many years preceding when I was at the Bar, I have never heard', added his lordship who went on to state, he was not there to in any way dictate to the Grand Jury, but he would say that nowhere did he see, outside Gilbank's own statements against himself, any evidence whatever of the accused having struck a blow at any person.

It was alleged that he followed the harvesters out of the public house; he was full of fight and had a row with Fee in the high road, and it was alleged that he suggested to somebody that they should get some sticks. It was further alleged that Gilbank jumped out of a hedge and struck some person whom he thought to be Fee. Gilbank had no quarrel of any sort against Dunn. He had no argument with him in the public house, and apparently bore him no ill-will or any sort. The Grand Jury might, therefore, think that they could not find a true bill against Gilbank for the willful murder of Dunn. Supposing even if it came out that a stick with which he had intended to hit Fee, had struck and caused the death of another person, he thought the charge should not be greater than manslaughter. How Gilbank came to be committed for willful murder he could not imagine; he could not understand it all. The Grand Jury might find a bill against him for manslaughter on the ground that if the death was caused by a stick hitting one man or another, he was responsible for manslaughter.

Following the words of Mr Justice Bucknill the Grand Jury found 'no bill' in the case of Harry Gilbank and he was discharged a free man. James Fee, aged 26 years, pleaded not guilty to the manslaughter of Edward Dunn at Bishop Burton on 19 September, and Mr Robertson, who prosecuted for the Crown, intimated that as the Grand Jury had thrown out the bill against Harry Gilbank, it was not proposed to offer any evidence against Fee.

The Grand Jury formally returned a verdict of not guilty, and his lordship, in discharging Fee, said that he only desired to say that worse things might happen to people that get into drink. If Fee had been sober this would not have happened.

Chapter 24

A Seaside Scrap! –
Frederick Thompson (1894-1928)

For many years Scarborough supported a number of pleasure boats which sailed out of the harbour and plied along the coast providing trips for visitors to the resort. Two in particular were operated out of the seaport itself, while a third, the *Yorkshireman*, built at Hull as a tug in 1928, sailed out of Bridlington harbour and plied between there and Scarborough each day during the summer season (Figure 90).

The two pleasure boat companies that operated from Scarborough, were the Scarborough Cruises Ltd, a company formed in the 1920s by fisherman and amusement operator Mr T W Round which by the 1930s was running the two boats, the twin-screw *White Lady II* and the original *White Lady* (Figure 91) and a Middlesbrough company which operated the *Bilsdale* from this port each summer season from 1924 with a Middlesbrough crew (Figure 92).

For a period, the *Bilsdale*, built as a tug in 1900, was the only big pleasure boat at Scarborough and the only competition for the local fishermen offering trips around the bay in their much smaller craft. She could carry many passengers in comparison, and was licensed for 386 persons. That, and her extra attraction of being a paddle-steamer meant that she drew a large share of the visitor custom, even when joined by the locally owned big pleasure boats. And there were those among the Scarborough harbour community who were angered by this 'outsider' pushing in to cream off 'their' business!

The animosity festered and eventually boiled over late on the night of Monday, 27 August 1928 towards the seaward end of the middle pier, where the *Bilsdale* was customarily moored.

Just before midnight there was a fight on the pier, involving two Scarborough fishermen and *Bilsdale* crewmen. This culminated in a deckhand of the latter boat, Frederick Thompson, aged 34, of Middlesbrough, being knocked into the harbour. Thompson ought to have suffered no more than a ducking in the harbour waters, but he had the ill-luck to fall heavily on to a small platform protruding from the hull of the *Bilsdale* before then dropping into the sea and sinking.

Figure 90. *The* Bilsdale *approaching Scarborough harbour.*

Figure 91. *One of the many pleasure craft captains who commanded the numerous craft that sailed between Bridlington, Scarborough and Whitby.*

To their credit, the two Scarborough men joined some of Thompson's mates in going to his rescue, but it was some little time before he was found and hauled out. The fatally injured crewman was rushed to hospital were he died a few hours later. The two Scarborough fishermen were then taken into custody and charged with his murder.

The preliminaries at Scarborough proved to be a gripping affair, and the public gallery at the Borough Court was filled with members of the fishing community for the weekly court appearance of the men. When the Magistrates eventually heard the case, surprisingly

Figure 92. *The* White Lady *pleasure boat taking visitors out to HMS* Hood.

they threw out the murder charge, reducing it to manslaughter, and sent the two men to stand trial at York Assizes.

Following their trial at York, the two Scarborough fishermen were found guilty, but the judge was apparently quite impressed by the two, at one point referring to their 'very decent' characters. And he clearly took the view that a number of those participating in the affray were 'in drink' as he put it.

The fishermen who had by this time spent five weeks in custody while on remand, were given sentences of being bound over to keep the peace for three years, and a lecture by the judge about keeping off drink in the future.

The *Bilsdale* continued to operate from Scarborough for another half-dozen summers and was finally broken up after her 1934 season there.

Chapter 25

The Vine Street Murder –
Mrs Mary Comins (1910-43)

On Monday, 22 March 1943, Thomas Johnson, aged ten years old, was playing with his two brothers in the disused garage at the former Vine Street Bus Station, when he was surprised to find a 'lady' lying in the vehicle inspection pit set into the floor. Alarmed, he ran home to his mother at 12 Trafalgar Street and told her of his discovery. Thinking it a fairy story, she assured him that he had 'seen a dummy, not a lady.'

After his tea the following Wednesday, Thomas returned to the garage premises and invited a young girl, Irene Hilda Mayes, who lived at 10 Vine Street, to 'have a look at the dummy' (Figure 93). Realising it was a dead body, she ran to tell Bobby Wood, aged sixteen, of 9 Vine Street, who dashed to the police station on Castle

Figure 93. *Vine Street, Scarborough, as it is today.*

Road. Sergeant Halford accompanied the youth back to the garage where, in the inspection pit, he found 'the body of a young woman, fully-clothed, lying face downwards in three inches of oil and water.' A ninety-foot long mark across the garage floor indicated that the body had been dragged feet first to the pit before being dumped therein.

At six o'clock that night, Detective Inspector John Boynton, Police Constable Goode and Dr Noel Herbert, the Deputy Police Surgeon, arrived on the scene. Photographs were taken and the body was removed to the Mortuary on Trafalgar Street West. Identification proved an easy matter. The dead woman was named as Mary Elizabeth Comins, aged thirty-three years, who had lived alone at 7 Wrea Lane (Figure 94).

Figure 94. *Wrea Lane, part of which was later demolished and redeveloped.*

An attractive woman, she had been employed as an assistant in the grocery shop of Jordan and Sons, in Prospect Road. Her husband Jack was then serving overseas with the Eighth Army in North Africa. She had been reported missing three days before by her brother-in-law, Eric Hill, of 6a Prospect Road, and her friend Mrs Edna Tyson, of 1 Wrea Lane, at 10.55 pm on 22 March.

Seemingly, Mary Comins and her friend Edna Tyson had spent the Sunday evening of 21 March in a local public house in the company of two soldiers, a corporal named Jimmy and a private called Dick, who said they were stationed at Pickering. In her statement to the police, Edna said the four of them had separated at around ten o'clock that night, but she had seen Mary Comins talking to a man on Dean Road, opposite the end of Wrea Lane an hour later.

Following a five-hour post mortem of Mary Comins' body on 26 March by Dr Peter Lindsay Sutherland, Professor of Forensic Medicine at Leeds University, his findings were 'no finger marks on the body, fracture of the lower jaw and death from asphyxia caused by manual strangulation'. To enable him to issue a Burial Order for the corpse, the Borough Corner, Claude Royle, held a preliminary inquest on 27 March 1943. It was adjourned pending police enquiries.

Within twenty-four hours the Scotland Yard Murder Squad were called to take over in the form of Chief Inspector Arthur Thorpe and his assistant, Sergeant Albert Griffin. The latter was later to rise to the rank of Detective Chief Superintendent and to become a leading figure in the Christie murder inquiry. Between them and with the assistance of the local constabulary, they interviewed numerous local residents and suspects and countless witnesses who claimed to have heard screams in Vine Street at about midnight on Sunday, 21 March.

It was quickly established that the garage premises had only been vacated by the military on the day before Mary Comins' body had been found. Every serviceman stationed at Scarborough was questioned regarding his movements on the night and day of 21-22 March - a marathon task for the police force because at that time the town was virtually an army camp with a great deal of troop movement going on.

By early April of that year, the search for Mary's killer or killers was widened to the south of England, in particular to certain units of troops who had been transferred from Scarborough, on or after that date. Eventually, 'Jimmy' and 'Dick' were traced, and interviewed by Chief Inspector Thorpe, and then exonerated.

Despite the two servicemen being cleared of any blame, it was generally assumed that a soldier was responsible for Mary Comins murder. Many local people believed that the police thought they knew the guilty man, but could not find sufficient evidence to bring a case against him.

Police inquiries were still continuing and no arrest had been made on 7 May when the Coroner's Inquest was resumed. After hearing all the available evidence, the Jury returned a verdict of 'Murder by person, or persons, unknown.' The killer was never traced. One theory is that the murderer was a local soldier who was then killed in action, taking his gruesome secret to his death.

In time, the garage was bought by Crystal, and in August 1995 the premises were put on the market at a price of £150,000. The sale of the garage was to herald a move to Seamer Road where a new parts and service centre was built, which became Crystal Ford, and is today Crystal Polar. The actual pit, however, in which Mary Comins body had been discovered was filled in some years previous to the move, in January 1972.

Chapter 26

The Marske Murder –
Mrs Linda M. Cook (1941-63)

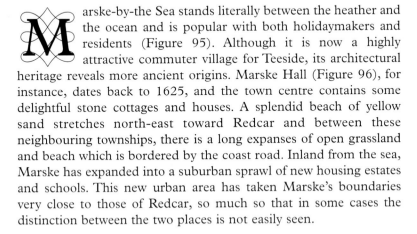

arske-by-the Sea stands literally between the heather and the ocean and is popular with both holidaymakers and residents (Figure 95). Although it is now a highly attractive commuter village for Teeside, its architectural heritage reveals more ancient origins. Marske Hall (Figure 96), for instance, dates back to 1625, and the town centre contains some delightful stone cottages and houses. A splendid beach of yellow sand stretches north-east toward Redcar and between these neighbouring townships, there is a long expanses of open grassland and beach which is bordered by the coast road. Inland from the sea, Marske has expanded into a suburban sprawl of new housing estates and schools. This new urban area has taken Marske's boundaries very close to those of Redcar, so much so that in some cases the distinction between the two places is not easily seen.

Figure 95. *Marske-by-the-Sea, Cleveland, formerly in the North Riding.*

Figure 96. *Marske Hall, front elevation.*

Like Marske, Redcar was once a fishing village (Figure 97). It has now grown into a busy and interesting seaside resort with a magnificent beach of firm sands, a fine promenade, well-patronised racecourse, good shopping and excellent leisure facilities that are popular with the people of Teeside. Like Marske, it has expanded so that it now merges with industrial Teeside along with surrounding villages and towns such as Coatham and Dormanstown. Even so, fishermen still operate from Redcar beach, resting their boats high on the sands when not at sea. Redcar's strong links with the ocean are evident in the Zetland Lifeboat Museum on the seafront that

Figure 97. *Redcar, once a small fishing community.*

Figure 98. *The corner of Newcomen Street and Newcomen Terrace as it is today.*

contains the oldest lifeboat in the world.

Side by side on the bracing North-East coast, the townships of Redcar and Marske were once part of the North Riding of Yorkshire. Today, they are in the county of Cleveland having been transferred into this new administrative county in 1974. Between the two townships is a railway line that runs inland from Redcar Station, passing through suburban streets on its route to Marske. As it nears the latter, this railway line forms a positive dividing line between the two communities, and stretching alongside this railway as it enters Marske, is Green Lane which also stretches between Marske and Redcar.

It was here, at the Marske end of Green Lane that the body of an attractive young woman was found in the autumn of 1963. She was strangled, dying from asphyxiation, and her killer has never been found.

Her name was Linda Margaret Cook, who was twenty-two years of age, and had lived with her husband Michael, in a flat in Kirkleatham Lane, Redcar. It was above the doctor's surgery where Linda was employed as a receptionist. She and Michael Cook, an insurance agent in the district, had been married for two years before they had separated. Mr Cook had gone to live in lodgings in Queen Street, Redcar, while Linda moved into another flat at 7 Newcomen Terrace, Redcar (Figure 98). She had moved into those premises on Friday 20 September 1963.

Figure 99. *The railway line which runs beside Green Lane crossed by the road bridge.*

It was two days later that she was found dead in Green Lane at 7am on Sunday 22 September by the driver of a milk lorry.

Detective Superintendent Albert Websdale and Detective Inspector Arthur Taylor of the North Riding Constabulary were put in charge of the murder investigation and immediately visited the scene. Two facts were rapidly established; Mrs Cook had not been subject to any sexual assault, and the absence of signs of a struggle at the scene suggested she had been murdered elsewhere.

The lorry driver who found Linda told how he had made his discovery. The body was lying by the roadside at a place where Green Lane lies below the level of the road, almost adjacent to a stone road bridge which spanned the railway. (Figure 99). The exact position was noted as lying on the verge of Green Lane a yard or two from the railway boundary fence and not far from a plate-layer's cabin, and at about one hundred yards from the A174 road which then ran nearby before it was diverted. He had the impression that it had been placed in that position after death because the long grass surrounding the body was undisturbed. Her clothes were neatly arranged too, suggesting the killer had placed her in what appeared to be a sleeping position. Had the murder occurred there, or had there been a struggle at the scene, disturbances to the grass would have revealed this.

When the body was found, Linda was wearing a pink woollen two-piece suit with a tight-fitting or pencil-slim skirt, and black leather court shoes with stiletto heels.

As the body was removed for post-mortem examination that revealed it was asphyxiation that had caused her death, the investigation team set about interviewing everyone who knew the young vivacious redhead. It was quickly established that she had left a local hotel at about 2.30 pm on Saturday afternoon, and it was possible that Linda had called at a nearby corner shop soon afterwards to purchase corn beef. There the trail ended.

An appeal for information and witnesses was also launched in the local press in which DS Websdale invited anyone to come forward who might have seen Mrs Cook after 2.30 pm on Saturday 21 September until sometime late on the same night, or even into the early hours of Sunday morning before 7.00 am. But very little information was forthcoming.

The problem of filling in these lost hours, coupled with the possibility that she had been killed elsewhere and dumped in Green Lane, presented some difficulties to the investigators. There was a lack of clues and evidence, and so it was decided, by the Chief Constable that the more experienced skills and expertise of Scotland Yard were required. Two detectives from the Yard's Murder Squad were therefore called in. This was an unusual decision, and is probably the last time Scotland Yard was called in to assist this provincial police force. The two Scotland Yard officers were Detective Chief Superintendent William Tennent and DS Raymond Peling.

After intensive questioning of people in Redcar and Marske, her husband Michael Cook was swiftly eliminated from the enquiries. One witness, however, did provide some information as to the movements of the deceased. It was established that Linda had been seen shopping at 4.30 pm on Saturday afternoon. She was then wearing the clothes in which she had been dressed when leaving the hotel at 2.30 pm, namely a brown sheepskin jacket and blue jeans. Whilst engaged upon that shopping trip, she had carried her sheepskin jacket and had bought some groceries. These were later found at her new flat in Newcomen Terrace, indicating that she had returned to that address sometime Saturday evening and changed to go out into the outfit she was found dead in.

DCS Tennet appeared on local television to appeal for more of her contacts and friends to come forward. It was his opinion that Linda Cook had known her killer. While the gap of lost hours was narrowed slightly, it was still not sufficient to provide a positive lead in any direction. Bus conductors, railway employees, taxi drivers and others in public service were revisited and interviewed, and the local public houses, clubs and places of public resort were again visited and photographs of Linda passed around.

Another avenue of investigation opened with the realisation that the street-fair that followed Stokesley Show had taken place on the Saturday night of her death. This attraction was a magnet for young people from a great distance, consequently intense enquiries were launched to see whether Linda had visited Stokesley that Saturday.

Stokesley is a charming North Yorkshire market town some twelve miles from Redcar. Its annual agricultural show is the largest in the region, attracting more than 20,000 visitors, but like many events of this kind, there is more to attract youngsters than the livestock and agricultural exhibits and displays. Sideshows, music, bars and the whole panoply of entertainment are here during the show and fill the entire length of the town's wide main street for four days. Some seventy showmen attend and the normal shops in Stokesley close down during that period.

It was an immense task to determine whether Linda either alone or with friends or some special date, had visited the town on the Saturday night before her death was discovered. Although the Fair had departed, detailed enquiries were made at Stokesley and from those fairground personnel who had moved on. But this new line of enquiry produced nothing.

Another line of enquiry that was not publicised during the early stages of the investigation involved a study of Linda's detailed diary. She had kept a daily account of her activities and it included the names and places where she met friends, both men and women. Unfortunately, many of these meetings were recorded only by the Christian names of those she met. The police sifted through this diary with care, gradually tracing those who were featured regularly within its pages, but like other facets of this enquiry, it also produced nothing conclusive. The blue-covered diary was in her handbag which was beside her body when it was found. This in itself was perhaps a tantalising clue to the character of the killer, who must have been very cool and confident to spend so much time bringing the bag from wherever he or she had killed her at time when speed would be of the essence.

Eventually, it became evident to the police that someone, or perhaps several persons, were withholding vital information because the case had attracted such widespread publicity but had turned up so very little in the way of information. Apart from a possible unconfirmed sighting on a late night bus travelling on Route 71 between Dormanstown and Redcar where it was said she got off alone near to Green Lane, the lost hours in Linda Cook's life remained a puzzle.

How was it that a young woman with so many friends and acquaintances, who was so well known both because of her work at the doctor's surgery and in her private life, could avoid being seen by someone who knew her? And where did she spend that Saturday night? And with whom did she spend the evening after dressing up so carefully?

Following a reconstruction of Linda's last movements and widespread appeals in the local pubs, clubs, dance halls, cinemas and other public places, including the football match between Middlesbrough and Bradford at Middlesbrough's Ayrsome Park, and after publicity in the newspapers, on radio and television, some three hundred people did come forward with snippets of information. The police were grateful for this response, but Chief Superintendent Tennent of the Yard did express a feeling that among certain individuals there was a determined reluctance to assist the police with their enquiries.

As the investigation lengthened into October, it became clear that no new information was to be forthcoming. Every possible avenue of enquiry had been explored and exhausted but the teams of some twenty detectives continued to check and recheck the information already obtained. They continued with house-to-house enquiries showing Linda's photograph around Redcar but in the end, the investigation gradually ground to a halt. There were simply no more fresh leads to follow.

Finally, the police were left with the feeling that someone in Redcar or Marske was concealing the killer, perhaps unknowingly, and the Scotland Yard detectives returned to London leaving this Northern crime unsolved. The file remains open, however. There is still time for the killer of Linda Margaret Cook to be brought to justice.

Chapter 27

A Last Swim –
The Murder of Alfred Harland (1900-1965)

T he east coast resort of Scarborough is noted for its fun and frolics. And in common with many holiday towns relies on an influx of casual labour during the season. Tuesday 22 June 1965 was a pleasant summer's day and there had been a steady stream of bathers enjoying the facilities at the town's North Bay outdoor swimming pool (Figure 100). The pool closed at tea-time and once the last of the visitors had gone, the bath attendants, David Chapman aged twenty-three and eighteen year old Richard Makinson decided on finishing the day with a refreshing pint at the nearby *Scalby Mills Hotel* before going home (Figures 101 & 102).

Figure 100. *North Bay outdoor bathing pool, Scarborough, in 1960.*

Figure 101. Scalby Mills Hotel, *formerly a water-powered corn mill which burnt down in 1821. Rebuilt, it soon became a popular hotel with tea garden. In 1949 Scarborough Corporation took it over, and in 1960, a new* Scalby Mills Hotel *was built.*

Figure 102. *The 'Smoke Room'*, Scalby Mills Hotel, *before 1949.*

Both Chapman and Makinson were new to their summer jobs. For Chapman in particular the employment was most welcome, as he had been out of work for a long period and had got into financial difficulties. Indeed, he had only started work three weeks previous. Despite being on duty the following day, they stayed in the local bar until after last orders, by which time both lads had consumed large amounts of beer and were clearly drunk as they shouted and sang their way back to their respective homes in Scarborough.

The return journey took them back past the swimming pool and both men then made the fateful decision to go for a midnight swim. It had been nothing more than an innocent suggestion and they planned to ask Alfred Harland, the sixty-five year old caretaker, to let them in for a quick dip.

Harland's duties meant that he often worked well into the night during the holiday season, but despite their loud calls and knockings they were unable to attract his attention. In a joint decision they decided to scale the main gate and gain entry into the courtyard. The light in Harland's office was shining, but looking through the window they saw it was deserted. Later, it was established that Makinson told Chapman that they keys to the pool area were kept in this office and still keen on a moonlight swim, the pair broke into the office in search of the keys.

Chapman, the eldest of the two took the lead and smashed a window pane through which they both entered. Mistakenly, the men both assumed that Alfred Harland would be in the pool area, probably cleaning the changing-room. It was at this point that they now realised that if caught on the premises, they could be in for a lot of trouble. Chapman told Makinson to pull the grille down that partitioned the pool area from the changing-rooms. This meant that if Harland heard the men splashing about he would be trapped in the changing area and unable to see who was trespassing.

It was while young David Makinson was closing the heavy grille door that Chapman's natural curiosity began to get the better of him, and in looking round the office for the keys, his attention was drawn to the day's takings which were also kept in Harland's office. It seems likely that at this stage Chapman had only intended to break in for a swim, but because of his financial problems, the temptation of easy money became too much for him in his drunken state.

As Chapman pondered over how to get at the money, a noise was heard from the pool area and moments later Makinson rushed back to tell his friend that the caretaker, who had not been as they imagined in the changing area, was on his way back to the office.

Fearful at being apprehended, rather than immediately fleeing the premises, for some inexplicable reason, they decided to intercept old Mr Harland before he could reach the office.

Chapman entered the pool area unseen in its darken state, possibly with the intention of hiding. The only light came from the elderly caretaker's flashlight, but a moving shadow as Chapman tried to creep beneath the diving board alerted Harland to the intruder. It is unclear exactly what then occurred, but the end result was that Alfred Harland ended up face down in the swimming pool water where he was left by the two youths.

The body was discovered early next morning. At five o'clock the milk delivery arrived at the North Bay pool. The milkman sensed that something was wrong when he noticed the front door stood open. Cautiously he made his way inside until he spotted the opened safe. That stopped him, and the police were called who found the caretaker floating in the pool. It was quickly realised that foul play had ensued and a murder enquiry was set up.

Despite their undoubted hangovers, and in the knowledge of their crime, the two pool attendants arrived at work as normal, no doubt with the intention of trying to brazen it out. Later that morning in the course of police enquiries Chapman and Makinson were interviewed by detectives. Unsatisfied with their accounts, the police took them both into custody, where each made a statement about the events of the previous night.

Richard Makinson's account suggested that Chapman had deliberately pushed Harland into the swimming pool with the intention of drowning him. They had then pulled the man's body from the water, removed his keys and gone back into the office, whereupon his friend had taken the money from the safe. What Makinson had done, as the police pointed out, was to accuse his colleague of murder during the course of a robbery, a crime that if proved, could be enough to send Chapman to his death at the hands of the executioner.

David Chapman, however, told a different story. According to his account, he was beside the swimming pool when Alfred Harland spotted him. The old man had then lunged at him with the possible intention of catching hold, missed, and then thrown a punch that caused Harland to lose his balance, and as he fell into the pool he knocked his head against the base of the diving board.

Harland's semi-conscious body came to the surface of the water. Chapman said he saw his arms move. 'He was struggling for a second. I didn't know whether he could swim. He seemed to go limp in the water'. Chapman then told detectives that he had then panicked and pushed the body away from him as he made his escape. Officers interviewing the man, however, noticed the coldness with which he described events and surmised that there was more to the story.

Chapman the went on to recount how moments later, Makinson had arrived at the pool side and realising what they were doing was wrong, demanded that they both fish the old man out of the water. Chapman told how they had then tried to save Harland:

We put him on the side of the pool on his back. I tried to feel a pulse and there wasn't one. I put my hand close to his mouth to see if he was breathing and I couldn't detect any breath. I didn't see his chest moving. I didn't se any white froth coming from his mouth. I thought he was dead.

Describing the next sequence of events, Chapman said,

We went back to the office. Makinson opened the safe with the key [which was taken from the caretaker's body]. *There were three cash bags. I opened one and passed one to Makinson, which he opened. I opened a third and Makinson went out.*

David Chapman concluded his statement by claiming that Makinson had gone back to the pool and on his return had said that he had dumped the old man back in the water. Giggling drunkenly, Makinson had told him, 'I've put Alf back'.

While the two men were being interviewed at Scarborough Police Station, the Home Office pathologist, Dr D Hainsworth, who had arrived that morning from Leeds University, carried out a post-mortem on the corpse. He noted that as the body had been removed from the water a copious amount of white foam had come out of the nose and mouth. Dr Hainsworth examined the head and found cuts and bruises on the man's scalp, but they were not serious, but he did state that the caretaker had been struck from above and found evidence of blows. There was a bruise above the right eye. He concluded his report by stating that the cause of death was by drowning, adding that Harland was in poor health; had already had a heart-attack and the doctor believed he could have suffered another at any time.

In October 1965 Chapman and Makinson appeared at Leeds at the Yorkshire Assizes before Mr Justice Havers. Together they were charged with capital murder. Both pleaded not guilty to the murder charge, but guilty to charges of breaking and entering and theft of over £50 in cash. The courtroom was packed and the atmosphere solemn.

The case for the prosecution as outlined by Mr John Cobb, QC, was that Chapman had struck Alfred Harland repeatedly near the pool and then pushed him away as he tried to make his escape. Afterwards Makinson, realising that the old man was alive, threw him back in the pool, knowing this would almost certainly finish him off. Mr Cobb submitted that both men had had a hand in the caretaker's death and therefore were both equally guilty of capital murder.

Mr Peter Stanley-Price, QC, defending Chapman, asked his client, 'Did you push him at all?'

The emphatic reply was, 'No, sir'.

Richard Makinson was defended by Mr Rudolph Lyons, QC. On the third day of the trial he called his client into the witness box and asked, 'Did you kill Alfred Harland?'

'No, sir', Makinson replied.

Mr Lyons probed further. 'Did you play any part in his death?'

Again the same answer.

Makinson then told the court he had no criminal record and had worked at the pool for six months. He had a good work record and had liked Mr Harland. He admitted drinking between six and nine pints of beer on the night in question and that he was drunk. He denied there was any premeditated design to break in for the purpose of robbery and said that they had just felt like a swim.

He told the court that when Chapman instructed him to pull down the grille, he thought it was to be a practical joke on the old man. The pulling-down of the metal grille made such a racket that it was this that had alerted Alfred Harland who came running toward him. Makinson said how he had turned tail and said to Chapman, 'Let's get out and come back later'.

The defendant claimed he escaped and once in the street looked back and saw Harland peering over the wall. 'I saw Dave was speaking to Harland... I did not think anything wrong was going on'.

Then, cursing his erstwhile friend, he told how he saw Chapman on the diving board pushing the elderly caretaker back into the water as the old man struggled to the surface. He told the court that he shouted Chapman to stop, calling out, 'Pack it in... what the hell did you do that for?'

Chapman was alleged to have replied, 'Shut up. We've got what we came for'.

This last statement was crucial, since according to Chapman's own evidence, the pair had supposedly up to this point not stolen the money. Makinson also alleged that Chapman had then looked coldly at him and said, 'I had to do it – he recognised me'.

Finishing his evidence, Makinson claimed he had only helped to throw Harland's body back into the swimming pool out of fear of Chapman.

In cross examination by Mr Stanley-Price, Makinson was asked why he had shared the proceeds of the robbery. 'I don't know. We just agreed to split it', he replied quietly.

Counsel defending Chapman continued by pointing out that although Richard Makinson had claimed he had seen his client pushing a drowning man back into the water, he was an accomplice and very drunk and the court must not rely too much on this evidence. He also pointed out that the robbery was not preconceived but was a spur of the moment weakness.

Making his final speech for the Crown, Mr Cobb stated that there could be no doubt that this was a grave and dreadful case, 'reflecting a degree of callousness and brutality the like of which one would fail to believe would be within the capacity of a human being'. He conceded that Makinson was a man of previous good character, but that he had indirectly at least participated in the night's violence and had been quite content to share the proceeds of the robbery. On the question of drunkenness, Mr Cobb said firmly, 'Drink is no defence... I would ask you to consider whether he is not using drink as something of a shield'.

In his summing-up, Mr Justice Havers commented first, with reference to Makinson, that there was no criminal offence in failing to help a drowning man. Addressing the jury, he then said.

Where there is a conflict of testimony between one or more of the witnesses for the prosecution... or defence, it is for you [the jury] *to decide which you accept.*

Finally, the judge posed the question of whether the men were working in concert or whether one of them could have genuinely not known that the other intended murder.

The jury then retired to consider the case. Two-and-a-half hours later they returned with their verdict. Chapman was found guilty of capital murder, while in the case of Makinson, they found him not guilty of any involvement in the murder of Alfred Harland but they found him guilty of being an accessory after the fact of grievous bodily harm. Richard Makinson was put on probation for two years.

When it came to sentencing David Chapman, there was a deathly hush in the courtroom as the black cap was draped upon the head of the judge. Addressing the prisoner, Mr Justice Havers told Chapman,

The jury, upon abundant evidence, have found you guilty of a callous and brutal murder... The sentence of the court upon you is that you suffer death in the manner authorised by law.

Outside the court, Chapman's wife, Margaret, burst into tears as she learnt of the sentence. During the trial it had emerged that Chapman had a criminal record for acts of violence. In November 1959 he had been convicted of actual bodily assault, and in May 1962, he had served a term in Borstal for a similar offence.

Although Chapman did not appeal against his conviction, on 9 November 1965, he was formally reprieved when the *Murder (Abolition of the Death Penalty) Act* received royal assent. His sentence was commuted to one of life imprisonment.

Finally, to conclude, while in many respects this crime was just another of the sort found enacted many times over in one variation or another throughout the land and throughout the centuries, one aspect of this case, however, makes it unique in the annals of criminal history – David Stephen Chapman was the last man in Great Britain to be sentenced to death for murder.

Notes and References

1. Young, Reverend George, *History of Whitby*, Volumes I & II. 1817.
2. For more detailed information see 'The Roman Fort at Huntcliff', by W. Hornsby and R. Stanton, *Journal of Roman Studies*, Volume 2, Pt 2, 1912. This also contains 'Notes on the Roman Coast Defences of Britain, especially in Yorkshire' by Professor Haverfield, LL.D, D.Lit. Also Mary Kitson Clark, *Gazetteer of Roman Remains in East Yorkshire*.
3. The various finds at Goldsborough – coins, pottery, sherds, bronze bracelets, jet finger rings, fragment of woollen cloth etc. – were presented to the Whitby Museum, and are there displayed, with photographs of the excavated foundations. There is also a small model giving a conjectural restoration of the signal station.
4. Loosely translated it means 'unlucky circumstances'.
5. *Scarborough Gazette*, 8 November 1894.
6. Charlton, Lionel, *A History of Whitby and Whitby Abbey*. 1779.
7. The words on the plaque read - *North Riding of Yorkshire County Council. From time immemorial at or near this place in Whitby harbour the ceremony of the Horngarth popularly known as the Planting of the Penny Hedge as been performed each year on the morning of the Eve of Ascension Day.*
8. Peacock, *Yorkshire Catholics*.
9. Fallow, T M 'Yorkshire Plate and Goldsmiths', *Archaeological Journal*, Volume LXI, No.241.
10. Jeffrey, Percy Shaw, *Whitby Lore and Legend*. 1923.
11. Walker, Peter, *Murders and Mysteries from the North York Moors*.
12. Jeffrey, Percy Shaw, *Whitby Lore and Legend*. 1923.
13. L Toulmin Smith (Editor) *The Itinerary of John Leland in or About the Years 1535-43*, Vol.1 1907.
14. Charlton, Lionel. *A History of Whitby and Whitby Abbey*. 1779.
15. Meadley, C., *Memorials of Scarborough*, p.151. 1890.
16. *ibid*, p.167.
17. Whitworth, Alan., *Aspects of Sleights*. 1999.
18. Planey, Colin de *Dictionnaire Infernal*. 1818.
19. *Secrets Merveilleux de la Magic Naturelle et Cabalistique de Petit Albert*, 1772.
20. Walker, Peter, *Murders and Mysteries from the North Yorks Moors*.
21. First recorded mention made by Petrus Mamoris in the fifteenth century.
22. Meadley, p.112.
23. *ibid*, p.172,173.
24. *Hull Packet*, 3 February 1823.
25. *York Courant*, 31 December 1822.
26. Dykes, *Smuggling on the Yorkshire Coast*, p.25. Dalesman Publishing Company, 1978.
27. *Hull Packet*, 12 August 1817.
28. Dykes, p.26.
29. *Hull Advertiser*, 30 July 1830.
30. *Bridlington Gazette*, 27 August 1909.
31. *Bridlington Free Press*, Friday 20 August 1909.

Aspects *of the*
Yorkshire Coast

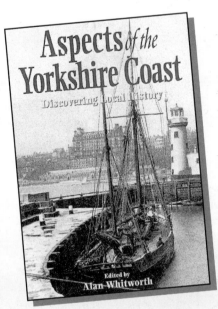

ISBN: 1·871647·54·1   £9.95

ISBN: 1·871647·79·7   £9.95

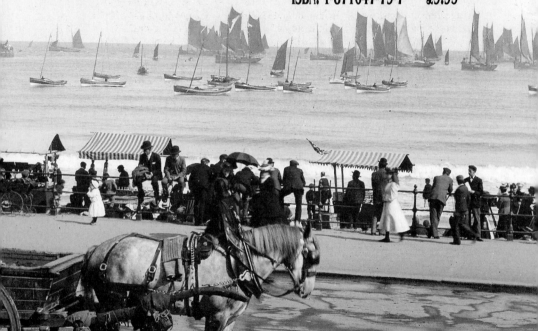

GENERAL INDEX